my mess is a bit of a life

Georgia Pritchett is a multi-award-winning comedy and drama writer. Her writing and production credits include *Veep*, *Have I Got News for You*, *Smack the Pony*, *Miranda*, *The Thick of It* and many more. She is currently a writer and co-executive producer on HBO's critically acclaimed show *Succession* and the creator and showrunner of *The Shrink Next Door*, starring Will Ferrell and Paul Rudd. She has five Emmys, five Writers' Guild Awards, a Golden Globe, a Bafta and a Trampolining Proficiency Level 1 Certificate.

georgia pritchett

my mess is a bit of a life

adventures in anxiety

faber

First published in 2021
by Faber & Faber Limited
Bloomsbury House
74–77 Great Russell Street
London WC1B 3DA

This paperback edition first published in 2022

Typeset by Faber & Faber Limited
Printed and bound by CPI Group (UK) Ltd, Croydon, CR0 4YY

A CIP record for this book
is available from the British Library

ISBN 978–0–571–36590–6

2 4 6 8 10 9 7 5 3 1

To all the hamsters I've loved and lost

For The Speck, The Scrap, The Moose,
The Witch and The Patriarchy

Prologue

As a very last resort, before I chose how to make my exit from the world, I decided to see a doctor.

'My mess is a bit of a life right now,' I mumbled. 'I mean, not that . . .'

She indicated that I should elaborate. But I couldn't. I couldn't speak. The words wouldn't come. They were there but they were out of my reach. She referred me to a therapist.

I went and I said nothing. I didn't know what to say, I didn't want to say anything and even if I did want to say something, the alien and the moths and Godzilla and the Dark Overlord Beaver made it impossible.

After weeks of silence, I was losing hope.

Her: How are you?
Me:

I tried to speak, but the moths were flapping furiously in my brain, the alien was pounding on my chest, Godzilla was stomping all over my inner Tokyo and the Dark Overlord Beaver was tucking into my intestines.

Her: Can you tell me what's going on?
Me:

The moths began bombarding and ricocheting inside my skull, the alien had acquired some kind of enormous mallet, Godzilla was roaring and obliterating my inner Tokyo and the Dark Overlord Beaver was now gorging on my innards.

Her: Can you tell me how you're feeling?
Me:

The moths suddenly stopped flapping, the alien stopped mid-pound, Godzilla stood, helicopter drumstick in hand and foot hovering over a building, the Dark Overlord Beaver put down my lower intestine. They all cocked their heads and listened to what I was going to say next.

Her: Are you anxious about anything?

I nodded.

Her: Can you tell me some of the things that worry you?

I shook my head.

Her: Maybe you could write them down . . . ?

And so I did.

my mess is a bit of a life

We're all doomed

My earliest memory is of sitting in my buggy in the snow. I was three. My mum said to my brother, 'Don't fall over in the snow.' Then my brother fell over in the snow.

This made me realise:

1. Bad Things happen.
2. Bad Things happen even if you tell the Bad Thing not to happen.
3. We're all doomed.

Who am I?

One day at nursery, my dad came to collect me. I remember looking up from my crayoning and seeing him at the door. I waited to be called but nobody called me. Finally, when all the other children had gone, I was allowed to leave.

As we walked home, Dad explained that when the teacher asked him who he had come for, he couldn't remember my name.

So instead he described me.

'She's small.'

The teacher said he'd have to narrow it down.

'She's small with curly hair.'

The teacher said he'd have to narrow it down some more.

In the end, the best he could come up with was 'Emily's friend'.

After that I worried that I wasn't really me. I worried that I was a different friend of Emily's and nobody had noticed.

In the event of my death . . .

When I was little, I used to worry that I would die in the night and that my family would not be able to manage.

So I would write notes with useful information like:

The peanut butter is in the cupboard with the broken handle.

Hammy likes to have sunflower seeds for breakfast.

We need more tiddlywinks because I ate them to see if they tasted like Smarties.

Tiddlywinks do not taste like Smarties.

Bad news

One day I arrived at nursery late. All the other children were there. My favourite place on the rug was taken – the one where you could hold a crayon against the radiator and watch while it melted.

As I unzipped my anorak, I realised that everyone in the room was singing 'We're Going to the Zoo'.

This sent me into total panic. I absolutely on no account wanted to go to the zoo with other children. Not now. I'd had no warning. I wasn't prepared. I had the wrong socks on. Also, since when did people deliver horrific news in the form of a song? It seemed inappropriate.

Could I run? Could I hide? I zipped my anorak back up and considered barricading myself in the Wendy house. As I crawled, sniper style, towards the plastic door, the children started singing 'Jack and Jill Went Up the Hill'. Now there's a song. Short, succinct and with a clear health and safety message. Why on earth were these people in favour of going to the zoo, when a mere trip up a hill caused one child to break his head and another to suffer from numerous undisclosed injuries? Luckily, after a quick burst of 'Humpty Dumpty' (who, let's remember, died from sitting on a *wall*), they wandered outside to play in the sandpit. They must have changed their minds about going to the zoo. Disaster averted.

Good news

I hated milk. One morning at nursery, the teacher told me I couldn't play with the other children until I had drunk my milk. Sometimes everything goes right. I didn't want to play with the other children AND I didn't want to drink my milk. I sat inside on the floor the whole day.

That was a good day.

The Patriarchy

We had a goldfish, a cat, a hamster and a tortoise – who hibernated all year round (so on reflection was probably dead) – but none of them would let me dress them up in my Snoopy's outfits or have tea parties with me. What we needed was a dog.

I really, really wanted a dog. My brother wanted a dog so he could train her to do tricks. My mum wanted a dog because she prefers them to humans. But my dad said NO. We were watching *Nationwide* at the time. The theme tune was like a dirge to my hopes. We pleaded but he declared he was going to have to Put His Foot Down.

The next day we got a dog. Flo lived for eighteen years. Dad said every time he looked at Flo, it reminded him of the Day He Put His Foot Down. This is why we have referred to Dad as The Patriarchy ever since. And this is why I have never Put My Foot Down about anything. Ever.

Love and marriage

Mum always claimed she'd married Dad for his money and was just biding her time until she found out where he'd hidden it. (Fifty-eight years later, he remains tight-lipped.) Sometimes, when I was walking Flo with my mum, a wedding car would pass and my mum would wave her arms and shout, 'Don't do it, you fools!' as it went by.

My mum never wore her wedding ring. But that might have been because I put it where the bulb goes in the lamp in the living room and when she switched the lamp on, it blew up.

Monsters under the bed

I used to worry about the monsters under my bed a lot.
Were they comfy enough? How could they sleep on a hard
floor surrounded by crumbs and dust? Sometimes I slept
under the bed so that they could have a turn on top.

Words

School was a hideous shock. For one thing, it was full of children and children are idiots. Loud idiots. It made me incredibly anxious. As I stepped into school, it was like being winded. I couldn't speak, I could barely breathe.

People would say I was shy. Teachers would demand that I speak. But the words just wouldn't come. They were there but they were out of my reach.

Tooth Fairy

I lost my first tooth biting into a toffee apple. I was alarmed but my mum tried to cheer me up by telling me about the Tooth Fairy. This was unwise. I was troubled by the concept of some weird old fairy breaking into my house while I was asleep and then taking body parts in exchange for money. It was the slippery slope. Where would it end? Was there an Ear Fairy? Was there a Toe Fairy? If I tucked my hand under my pillow while I was sleeping, would she take that? Sometimes at night, my head would end up under my pillow. And my head had teeth in it. Would she just take the whole thing? What was a fairy's load-lifting capacity? And why did nobody have the answers to the really important questions?

Different pillows

Sometimes we went to stay with Nan and Bok. This made me very anxious indeed. They had different pillows.

Nan wore shiny blouses and smelt of cupboards. Bok had a knee that clicked on the twelfth stair whenever he went upstairs.

As soon as we arrived, Nan would put us in the bath and scrub us clean. Then she would cut our hair with the kitchen scissors and then march us to the shoe shop to buy pinchy shoes.

I could never sleep at Nan and Bok's because I was too clean. And they had nylon sheets. And my too-clean body would just spin in the nylon sheets and I couldn't get comfy.

Sometimes Bok would come and tell me stories to help me get to sleep. It was too dark to see him. I could just see the glowing end of his cigarette.

My favourite stories were 'Naughty Georgie' stories. I loved these because not only was the Georgie in these stories naughty, but she didn't worry about it. She didn't worry about anything.

Jimmy

When I was four, I was given the record of Jimmy Osmond's 'Tweedle Dee' for Christmas. I also appeared in the Nativity play as Stable Door. God's appearance in my life coinciding with Jimmy Osmond's appearance in my life was a little confusing and, for a long time, I thought they were the same person. The same happened with Bob Dylan and Father Christmas.

Even as an adult I can't quite shake the image of God as Jimmy Osmond in a sheet.

This may be the problem I have with religion. Having a podgy pre-pubescent Mormon as a God isn't very reassuring. I mean, I love the song 'Tweedle Dee', but somehow I don't feel my fate is safe in his chubby, slightly sweaty hands.

Baby bird

I started writing before I could write. I would speak
stories into a tape machine in a breathy snotty voice.
They were all, without exception, about baby budgies who
fell out of nests and couldn't find their way home. It's a
niche genre. I would like to say that these stories have
been kept and treasured – but I'm pretty sure they got
taped over with Father Christmas singing 'Blowin' in the
Wind'.

Fluffy

When I was little I used to think that sheep were clouds
that had fallen to earth. On cloudy days I used to worry
that I would be squashed by a sheep.

Fame

Fame came early for me. The teachers at school informed my parents that some photographers had visited the school and I was going to be on the front cover of a book. They were very excited.

This was the book.

In answer to your question, no, I never did learn to adjust. And in answer to your other question, yes that is a yellow smock coupled with some green polyester flares.

Finding my voice

At school I spent every second of my time with My Best Friend David. We held hands all day.

I would wear my yellow polyester smock and my green polyester flares. He would wear a zip-up brown polyester cardigan and purple polyester flares. We were a highly flammable couple.

My Best Friend David was more confident than me. My Best Friend David didn't worry. My Best Friend David liked talking to people. My Best Friend David liked new things and adventure. My Best Friend David encouraged me to speak. He did this by teaching me to swear. But he explained that if we said a syllable each it wouldn't be so bad.

My Best Friend David: Fu
Me: king
My Best Friend David: No
Me: ra

Those were my first words at school.

Happy endings

When I was five, I asked for a pet canary. We got on the number 12 bus and went to the pet shop. I chose a green-and-yellow canary with a noble look in his eye. On the way home, we passed Nelson's Column. I realised Nelson must have been very important because he had a column and everything. So I decided Nelson was a good name for my canary.

I wish I could tell you Nelson was happy, but he didn't like being in a cage and he didn't like my cat or my dog. Soon his feathers started to fall out. He seemed listless and spent a lot of time at the bottom of his cage looking depressed. The noble look in his eye changed to a demoralised and defeated look.

One day I came home from school and the cage door was open and Nelson was gone. Mum told me that Nelson had escaped and had flown off and was probably living happily with a lady canary and had built a cosy nest somewhere. I missed Nelson but I was pleased for him.

A few years later I mentioned Nelson to The Patriarchy and said it was sad what had happened to him (meaning the feathers and the depression and the defeated look) and The Patriarchy said, 'I know, it was awful, I had to take him in the garden and club him to death with a brick. It took ages for him to die.'

'But I thought he escaped and found a lady canary and built a cosy nest?' I said, alarmed.

'Oh yes. That's right,' said The Patriarchy. 'That's what happened.'

This taught me that there's no such thing as happy endings.

Giants

Sometimes when we were going into the West End, we would walk to Elephant and Castle to get the Tube. To me, Elephant and Castle was a futuristic utopia. It had two giant roundabouts and a green shopping centre with an actual elephant on top. On one roundabout, a huge metal slab crouched which was definitely a UFO. I didn't like walking in the subways beneath the UFO because they smelt of wee and because that would almost certainly be where the aliens would hang about waiting to kidnap humans and experiment on them.

Near the other roundabout was one of many enormous new council estates. One had a play area near the road which was some sloped concrete, some giant concrete globes and then smaller concrete pillars jutting up from the ground which looked like teeth, with litter caught in the gaps. I had no idea how to play on this play area but I was intrigued. I made The Patriarchy stand for hours while I tried to solve the puzzle of the playground. There must have been a way of having fun, I just couldn't work out what it was.

More fun than the playground was the Tube. Riding on the squealing wooden escalator, walking down the long subways with hot wind blowing at you, waiting on the platform and hearing the distant roar thundering in the tunnel. I used to worry that it was a giant hurtling towards us. And then when the Tube arrived, all lights and noise and shrieking brakes, I would be a bit disappointed that it wasn't a giant.

Action Man

Our dog, Flo, had not delivered in terms of dressing up in my Snoopy's clothes and having tea parties. All my pets devoted most of their time to running away from me. This was disappointing.

My brother was not bothered about the animal exodus. He was too busy playing with his Action Man. I suddenly REALLY wanted an Action Man. An Action Man could not die (fish), hibernate (tortoise), move next door (cat), 'fly away' (canary) or devote his life to avoiding me (dog).

I begged my brother to give me one of his Action Man figures – so he gave me his old Action Man, which had one leg. The problem was, I wanted an Action Man with two legs. (I know, I know, on top of everything else I was a body fascist.) When it was my birthday I told everyone that I wanted a new Action Man because my old Action Man only had one leg, which meant that he couldn't get around very well. Bok assured me he had it covered.

On the day of my birthday, Nan and Bok handed me a package and I unwrapped it excitedly. This was my new Action Man! But no, inside the package was a small wheelchair which Bok had made out of wood. Now my Action Man could get around.

This taught me that adults are idiots.

The weather report

Mum has always had a complicated relationship with the weather. Every morning the first thing she does is to get the newspaper and look up the weather in every place she has ever been to – a bit like stalking an ex.

So, often, when I came down to breakfast, I was greeted with a furious 'You'll never guess what it's doing in Honfleur!'

And whatever it was doing was seen as some kind of personal provocation or betrayal.

Haiku

I went to a school where you only had to go to school if you felt it was right for you to go to school that day. Quite often I felt it was right for me to stay at home and play with the dog (much to Flo's horror).

When I did go to school, we spent a lot of time lying on the carpet or expressing ourselves through finger painting or plasticine. The closest I got to doing maths was when my teacher Jean sent me out to buy cigarettes for her and I had to come back with the right change. Sometimes my other teacher, Howard, took me home on the back of his motorbike.

Occasionally Henry, the headmaster, would gather us all together and would decide we were going to have A Proper Lesson. He would sometimes tell us about the plague or else about triangles. But usually he got us to write haikus. He seemed really determined that if nothing else we would leave primary school having mastered the Japanese tradition of short-form poetry.

Counting syllables
Is the only thing I learnt
When I was at school.

Mr Benn

I used to love watching *Mr Benn*. I never missed an
episode. This was because I hoped that one day, he would
not change into his outfit magically, and I might actually
get to see him in his pants. I never missed an episode.
But I never saw any pants. That's when I learnt about
disappointment.

Zoo

Granny and Grandpa lived near London Zoo. We used to go to the zoo a lot.

Whenever we went to the zoo, Granny would ask, 'Which was your favourite animal?'

And I would answer, 'The pigeons on the paths.' And then she would swear.

Robot

I used to worry that everyone else in the world was a robot and I was the only human. And if I let on that I knew this secret, they would kill me. When I told my brother this, he pretended to be a malfunctioning robot and then tried to kill me. I think anyone would have done the same in his position.

Cake

I didn't like parties when I was a child because, well, who really likes parties? But one time I came back from a party and to my parents' amazement, I said I had had a good time.

'Why?' they asked.

'I had cake and I didn't join in any of the games.'

This has very much been my approach to life.

Staying on the pavement

My brother Matthew was four years older than me and we used to go to school together. We would catch the bus, or sometimes the Tube, and walk the rest of the way hand in hand. I felt completely safe with him. As long as I held his hand and stayed on the pavement, I knew I would be all right.

My brother was the cleverest person I knew. He knew all about articulated lorries, he knew the rude version of 'We had joy, we had fun, we had seasons in the sun' and he could stick a liquorice string up his nose and make it come out of his mouth. I wished I could be like him.

One day, as we were walking home from school, we heard a loud hooting. We looked and saw a car driving along with a man sitting on the roof. The driver of the car did not look happy and was honking his horn repeatedly. The man sitting on the roof did not look happy either.

We watched the car pass, baffled, and as we carried on towards the bus stop, I suddenly felt my brother's hand yanked out of mine.

I turned and saw the man who had been on top of the car put his arm round Matthew's neck and drag him into the middle of the road. Then he shouted, 'If anyone comes near me, I'll kill him!' and he held a knife to his throat.

All the traffic stopped, all the noise stopped. I knew I wasn't allowed to step off the pavement without Matthew, so I stood at the very, very edge of the kerb and shouted his name.

I'm not sure how long I stood there, shouting, 'Matthew, Matthew, Matthew,' but I knew I couldn't go home without him and I knew I couldn't step onto the road, so I was paralysed.

Eventually a police car screeched up and four policemen jumped out and bundled the man to the ground. Matthew wriggled from the man's grip and rushed over to me and grabbed my hand. We ran to the bus stop and jumped on the bus and went home.

We didn't say much on the bus. When we got home, Matthew told Mum and Dad what had happened.

Then we all got the bus to school together. It was very strange to be heading back towards school as the sun was going down.

We didn't go to school, we went to a police station near the school. I was given some colouring to do while the police spoke to my brother and my mum and dad.

I wondered if the man was in the same building as us right now. Would he come and find us? I asked the policewoman if he was nearby. She said he was downstairs and he had taken all his clothes off and they were busy trying to persuade him to put them back on. I asked if he would go to prison and she said, 'Not prison, somewhere else.'

After this a policeman took us all to see the police horse. The police horse did a really, really long wee. We all watched, not knowing what to say.

Anxious Bear

My mum tried to help with my anxiety by buying me
a teddy – a companion, someone who I could tell my
worries to. But you only had to look at the bear to see
that he had some serious issues. His eyebrows were
knitted (in both senses), his little mouth was wonky
and his ears looked extremely perturbed. I named him
Anxious Bear. I tried to help him, but this was a bear
with multiple neuroses. He was fucked up. He was scared
of heights, scared of noises, scared of being alone, scared
of other people . . . he worried about illness, about death,
about a meteor hitting the planet. He was one high-
maintenance little ball of fur. It was *exhausting.*

Hammy

I loved my hamster. I loved my hamster more than
anything in the world. I loved my hamster so much it
hurt.

Hammy didn't seem to return my love. Even though I
moved Hammy from his small cage into a luxury wooden
bungalow (made for my wheelchair-bound Action Man by
Bok), he was always escaping.

He would be gone for weeks, but eventually I would
track him down and push him up the easy-access slope
into his bungalow again. He would stare out of the lattice
windows and gnaw at the door miserably. Sometimes I
would write him a tiny postcard and post it through the
letter box to cheer him up, but he would ignore it. Every
so often, he would somehow manage to open the door
from the inside and he would be off again.

One time he was gone for months and I thought I
would never see his little red eyes again. But then I went
to go to the loo and there he was swimming in the loo.

The problem was, I couldn't put my hand in the loo and
rescue him because there was wee in the loo. That's when
I realised there is no such thing as unconditional love.

(NB: My mum rescued him. And that's when I realised
my mum was not as concerned with personal hygiene as
she should be.)

Spam

I used to be scared of school lunches. There was so much noise and there were such strong smells and there was a lot of brown food. I would only ever eat Spam because that was pink.

A boy in my class would only eat custard. He used to be called 'Just custard' because that's what he would say. One day, the custard jug got knocked out of the Dinner Lady's hand and the hot custard poured onto his head. He had to go to hospital.

I stopped having Spam after that because I was worried I would be injured in a Spam-related incident.

Sweet

Apart from Spam and custard, my diet was somewhat limited when I was a child. I drank either lemonade or neat Ribena with breakfast, lunch and dinner. Breakfast would be Smarties, Jelly Tots or Spangles. Lunch might be a spoonful of peanut butter dipped in a jar of sugar. Then sherbet poured in lemonade for pudding.

The Patriarchy was an excellent cook. His other nickname was the Little Chef. He would try to tempt me with delicious food he had cooked. A curry which he had spent days preparing – grinding the herbs and spices and marinating the meat. Or maybe a miniature brunch – bacon cut up into tiny pieces next to fried quails' eggs and a tiny square of fried bread.

But I rejected all his culinary endeavours. My favoured dinner was 1p sweets – flying saucers, cola bottles, jelly foam mushrooms or maybe a Black Jack, if I was feeling sophisticated. Then for pudding, a chocolate milkshake but with only enough milk to make it into a paste.

The advantage of having a high-sugar diet is that you don't feel anxious for a while. Though you do get tummy aches and blurred vision.

Teeth

For some reason I had very bad teeth as a child. One day I had to have a tooth removed by the dentist. I worried about this A LOT. When I came round, I found out he had removed SIX teeth. He hadn't wanted to tell me because he thought I would worry. This taught me that when you are worried about a Bad Thing happening, the Bad Thing Will Probably Be Even Worse Than You Think It's Going to Be.

Emergency

When I was seven, my brother moved to secondary school and I started travelling to school alone. Every day, The Patriarchy would give me 2p for the bus journey to school, 2p for the bus journey home and 5p for emergencies.

When I got on the bus, the conductor would refuse to take my 2p and would give me 2p instead.

This meant that when I got off the bus, I had 11p to buy sweets with. Usually eleven jelly foam mushrooms. Or a packet of Spangles and one jelly foam mushroom. Or if it had been a difficult morning, a cigarette.

Then every day, when I came home from school, I would get to the bus stop and discover with horror that I had no money.

This is when I realised there are some emergencies you just can't plan for.

Cupboards

I didn't like cupboards as a child. I used to worry that
if I went inside, the cupboard might actually be a Time
Machine and it would take me back in time. From what
I'd gathered, history had nothing to recommend it.
Dinosaurs, wars and, worst of all, terrible loos. Or even
no loos. It didn't bear thinking about. I was grateful
that I lived in a time with the most advanced, futuristic,
cutting-edge technology – colour TVs, three channels,
SodaStreams and Dymo Label Makers, which were the
most space-age thing I had ever encountered. If only I
could have had one. Instead of a small wooden wheelchair
for my Action Man.

Spelling

One day I decided to Run Away From Home. My mother had done something terrible (I think she might have suggested I eat fewer sweets) so I decided enough was enough. I wrote a note, packed a bag and headed for the door.

I was halfway out of the door when I heard howls of laughter. They had found my note. This wasn't the reaction I had been expecting.

Regret, remorse, self-recrimination, yes. Laughter, no.

I tiptoed back to the living room.

Apparently I had written:

I hat you al – you hut my flings – I'm runin awa

This taught me that you must never attempt to do something you can't spell.

The lady on the bus

One day I was sitting on the bus counting out my sweet money. A kind-looking old man was sitting next to me. He looked a bit like Bok. Every so often he smiled at me.

Then a lady got on the bus. The old man swore at the lady. I was surprised to hear him using such words. The lady ignored him at first but then the man stood up and started telling her to go back where she'd come from. She asked him to leave her alone. But he wouldn't. She got off the bus and he followed her. There was a bomb site by the bus stop where I had played many times. She picked up a brick and threw it at him. It hit his glasses, which smashed. Everyone froze.

Her face was the saddest thing I had ever seen.

Scam

One year at Christmas, my brother told me that Father Christmas had made some changes to the whole stocking system and if I wanted to keep putting up a stocking, I had to pay £2.50 a year rental fee on the stocking. I did want to keep putting up my stocking, so I handed my brother the £2.50.

The following year, my brother informed me that Father Christmas was offering a deal. Three years of stocking rental for the bargain price of £7.50. Being a forward-thinking child (and rubbish at maths), I seized the opportunity and paid up.

The next year, my brother offered me the same deal. I pointed out that I had paid last year. My brother said Father Christmas had no memory of this. I was very upset. My brother shrugged and said he was just telling me what Father Christmas had told him.

This is when I realised that you don't get anything for free and also that Father Christmas is a complete and utter bastard. I know he's written some great songs, but even so.

Underground

At weekends, I would visit my best friend David in his flat. He had a dad with a severe stammer. It was unusual to meet someone who had more trouble speaking than I did.

David and I would run around his estate, ringing doorbells and dashing away. There were cranes and bulldozers everywhere. They were in the midst of building hundreds of flats in the Barbican. David and I would slip through railings and sneak into underground cities beneath these half-built flats. We scurried along empty passages, squeezed through tunnels, ran with rats next to sewage pipes, entered half-built apartments, and played hide-and-seek in the gloomy airless concrete tombs under the enormous empty tower blocks. Usually we would get lost, fail to find the way we had come in, and roam around looking for an escape. Somehow David always managed to spot a loose door, a dark stairwell or a dot of sunlight and we would squeeze through and emerge back on the surface somewhere completely different. Then we would have to find our way back to his flat in the bright glare of daylight.

On other days, we caught a lift to the top floor of the tower blocks and climbed up the fire escape stairs to the roof. Then we'd stand on the roof, leaning into the wind, looking down at the tiny world below. Nobody ever stopped us or spotted us or even seemed to notice us. We were invisible. And that's how I liked it.

Men

Sometimes at school, David would go off and play Kiss Chase with the girls. Then I would sit in the secretaries' office and feel sad. It smelt of the ink from the old-fashioned photocopier in there.

Doreen, one of the secretaries, would look out of the window and tell me which girls he was kissing. Sheila, the other secretary, assured me all men were bastards.

Secrets

When I was about eight, I asked my friend why she was so much taller than me. She said casually, 'Well, that's because you're a dwarf. Haven't your parents told you that yet?'

I said they hadn't.

She said it was obvious. 'Why do you think you have such a big head?'

For about two years I was on tenterhooks, waiting for my parents to break the news to me. Finally I couldn't stand the suspense any longer. I sat my mum down and said, 'It's all right. I know the secret and I've come to terms with it. You don't need to worry.'

Mum looked at me blankly. 'What secret?'

'That I'm a dwarf. Veronica told me.'

Mum laughed for a long time.

'You're not a dwarf,' she said. 'But you *are* an idiot.'

This seemed like worse news.

Hymns

At primary school, we used to have Assembly once a
week. And every week, we would sing one of two hymns:
'My Ding-a-ling' by Chuck Berry or 'Jake the Peg' by Rolf
Harris. At least I thought they were hymns. I found out
they weren't during an RE lesson at secondary school.
That's when I got my first detention.

Roots

Flo was a West Highland terrier. Every year we went to Scotland because my mum said it was important for her to get back to her roots. In order to get there, we had to catch a bus, a Tube, an overnight train, a small train, a ferry and another bus.

Once we were there, we would walk and walk, discovering lochs and coves and heather-covered hills. Flo didn't seem that interested in her roots. Or in walking. Inevitably, The Patriarchy would end up carrying her. The smelly embodiment of the Day He Put His Foot Down would lick his resentful face all the way home.

More secrets

I did not like wearing shorts when I was little because I didn't want people to know I had knees.

Chimpy

Sometimes I would fight with my brother. We would play a game where we had to try to push the other one off the bed onto the floor. He always won.

I invented an alter ego for myself, called Chimpy. I was convinced that Chimpy had superhuman strength. Like the Incredible Hulk.

The fights went something like this:

'Ready? Go!'

Thunk (as I hit the floor).

'OK, you've beaten me, but here's Chimpy!'

Thunk.

'That was twin of Chimpy, this is the *real* Chimpy!'

Thunk.

'That was other twin of Chimpy, now this is the *real* Chimpy!'

Thunk.

This would go on for hours.

Eventually I realised I didn't have an alter ego with superhuman strength, I had an alter ego who was a bad loser.

Dusty legs

One day, Henry herded us all into the hall. I knew what was coming. Haikus. But no, he closed all the blinds so that it was very dark and announced that he was going to teach us 'the facts of life'. Then he showed us a film about bees.

The bee would visit a flower and get dusty legs. Then it would visit another flower and its legs would get more dusty. Then it would meet another bee with dusty legs. And then, well, it all gets a bit hazy, but somehow they had a baby bee. I'm not sure.

I liked David a lot but I did not want to get dusty legs.

Imaginary friend

I had a difficult relationship with my imaginary friend.
She was called Samantha and she was very sophisticated.
She had straight hair, she could blow bubbles AND she
could skip. If only I'd had straight hair or been able
to blow bubbles or skip, my life would have been very
different.

Samantha found my company tiresome. She was
usually too busy to play with me. She was always off
having fun with her other friends. Sometimes she'd
squeeze me into her hectic social life, but I worried she
was doing it out of a sense of duty and she wasn't really
enjoying herself. By the time I was ten, she'd stopped
showing up. She didn't even say goodbye.

Old Lady

Around this time, I became aware of the old lady who lived next door. We called her the Old Lady. She was so old it was scary. And she was so old she was stuck upstairs on the second floor and couldn't get downstairs. Sometimes she would throw 10p pieces wrapped in tin foil out of her window. It hurt when they hit you.

Sometimes she would throw the key out and I would go upstairs to see her. The room she lived in was full of old newspaper and furniture and blankets and a strange smell. There was nowhere to sit and I did not want to touch anything.

Her niece, who was also very old, lived downstairs in the basement. She didn't leave the house either because she was barmy.

One day I climbed over the fence between our gardens to see if I could catch a glimpse of the Barmy Niece. I pressed my face to the glass and looked inside. I expected to see the same squalor that filled the Old Lady's room. Instead it was completely empty apart from a mattress on the floor.

On the wall were some words written in huge letters. They said: **'The wages of sin is death.'**

They were written in some kind of dark red liquid. Let's decide it was paint.

That's when I discovered it's very hard to climb over a fence when your knees want to bend the wrong way.

Mrs Grumpy

I worried a lot that my parents would be killed in a car
accident and I would be an orphan. I used to keep a list
(that I would update) saying which parents I would like
to have if mine died. At the top of the list were Valerie
and Trevor because they had a car. Next were Rosemary
and Brian because they had a car too. I didn't think about
the fact that my parents not having a car made it less
likely that they would die in a car accident. Rosemary
was a Proper Mother. She used to say things like 'Once
funny, twice silly, three times a smack,' and 'We're not at
home to Mrs Grumpy.'

The Voice of God

I used to think that when you went to the theatre, the loud boomy voice that told you to take your seats and also told you about ice cream was the Voice of God. I like the idea of the Almighty being concerned about refreshments.

Sealink

When we stayed with Nan and Bok, we used to drive to Eastbourne, park the car on the seafront and watch the Sealink ferry arrive and leave again while they drank tea from a tartan flask. This was our big day out.

One time, it was such a hot day that my brother and I begged to be allowed out of the car. Nan and Bok agreed so we picked our way painfully across the pebbles to the sea.

There I took off my new pinchy shoes that Nan had bought me, and my holey socks, and I rolled up my polyester trousers so that I could paddle. It was lovely in the water. My brother and I pottered about in the waves. But I wanted to get a bit deeper, where there were fewer rocks and less seaweed and litter. I edged further out and suddenly slipped. I remember very clearly seeing the horizon (and Sealink) disappear as I slid underwater.

I couldn't swim. I felt myself sink to the bottom. I was definitely going to die. That was not what I had been planning.

Suddenly, hands pulled me up. My brother had grabbed me and he dragged me to the shore.

I looked up to Nan and Bok. Was I in trouble? Nearly dying was the sort of thing that Nan would not approve of. Nan was not one for showing emotion, so it was rather startling to see her crying. Crying with laughter.

Our day was cut short. They didn't even get to drink their tea. I had to sit on their picnic blanket to avoid getting the car seat wet. We drove home and I thought about life and death while Nan continued to laugh.

Nine

When I was nine I felt very tired and achy. I didn't want
to go out. I wanted to stay at home all the time. And I
wanted to lie on my bed.

I was told I was growing.

I measured myself a lot. I didn't grow.

Blankets

I didn't like tea and coffee so instead I drank Lemsip with lots of sugar in it. I liked how it made me feel sleepy. I would find all the blankets in the house and put them on my bed. It was reassuring to feel the heaviness of the blankets.

For some reason I got a lot of tummy aches so to help with those I'd have a swig of kaolin and morphine. It was so chalky but I liked the way it made me shudder.

If I still felt anxious after that, I'd lean out of the window and have a cigarette. Far below me, the tortoise was a tiny speck in the garden. It hadn't moved in months.

Custody battle

My favourite toys were my Action Man in his wooden wheelchair (who I had grown to love), the Bionic Woman and a very realistic life-sized black baby who towered over Bionic Woman and Action Man. They made an unusual family.

Later Lindsay and Pete (Bionic Woman and Action Man) adopted another child, Starsky. This was a doll made on a much smaller scale than his freakishly large sister. Lindsay and Pete didn't mind, they were happy. For a while.

The trouble started when they were evicted from their bungalow to make way for Hammy. Around this time, Flo started having phantom pregnancies. She had been having a lot of sex with my toy sheep so it wasn't surprising. In the absence of a real puppy, Flo decided that Starsky was her puppy. She would steal Starsky and put him in her basket and lie on him and try to suckle him. I would then rescue him and return him to his anxious parents.

A lengthy and upsetting custody battle ensued.
Flo won.

Fearless

Kenny lived next door (on the other side from the Old Lady). He was a year older than me and he had lots of brothers and sisters and all their names began with K. There was Kevin and Kathy and Kim and Keith and Kelly. This seemed the height of sophistication to me.

I wished I could be like Kenny. He was fearless. There were rumours that he had burnt down the local church. They never found out who did it and Kenny would neither confirm nor deny it.

I wasn't ready to burn down churches but I was ready for some kind of entry level of being naughty. Kenny taught me to squeeze out of my bedroom window and scramble over the roofs of the houses. He taught me to climb to the very top of the conker tree and get the conkers nobody else could reach. He taught me to blow smoke rings. He was allowed to stay up much later than me. His bedroom was next to mine and sometimes I could hear him playing music late into the night. And sometimes I could hear him crying.

Messiah

When I was little I used to worry that I might be the Messiah. I really didn't want to be the Messiah because:

a) I'm bad at public speaking and I thought being the Messiah would probably involve a lot of that.

b) Germs make me very anxious and so I definitely don't want to touch sick people and I really don't want them to touch me.

c) I have a very low pain threshold and I can't help feeling that being the Messiah is going to end badly.

d) My frizzy hair would not work well in stained glass. Stained glass is a very unflattering medium.

e) I'm not sure about Eternal Life. It seems like life is long enough already.

There is nothing to fear but fear itself. And also Daddy Long Legs

I always used to worry about Daddy Long Legs flying into my hair and getting tangled up. And then flying off and leaving some legs behind in my hair. Nobody wants legs in their hair.

Then Veronica told me that they were actually the most poisonous insects on earth, but that their jaws are too weak to bite you. After that I worried that they might gang up and lick me to death.

Memories

Kenny broke his leg. He let me borrow his crutches. I spent six weeks walking with his crutches. After a while, I couldn't remember who had broken their leg. Was it me or Kenny?

Kenny said he had heard one of the other boys ask one of the other girls to touch his willy. And she did.

'You saw it too, didn't you?' he asked me.

I nodded.

Moments later, we heard adults shouting and doors slamming and then an eerie silence.

The girl's mum came and asked me if I had really seen what Kenny said. I tried really hard to think, but I couldn't tell if I had seen it or if Kenny had just told me I'd seen it.

Conkers

Every autumn, kids would come and climb the conker tree near our house. And every autumn, at least one would slip and fall. They weren't experts like Kenny and me. One of our neighbours was a doctor and he would tend to the children until the ambulance arrived. I saw cracked heads and broken limbs. One day, a boy impaled his leg on the railing. He extricated himself and then hopped over to our doorstep, where he bled profusely. When the ambulance had taken him away, the doctor came and threw a bucket of water over the step to wash the blood away. But he left a little bit of leg behind.

Asking for it

When I was ten, I bought a falconry glove at a jumble sale. It was far too big for me but I loved it. I wore it all day every day. I thought it made me look really cool. Like a king. Or a spy. Or Snoopy. It did not make me look cool. And it made picking up Jelly Tots very difficult indeed. Thank God large birds of prey did not start landing on my arm. That would have been terrifying, but the way I was dressed, I would have been asking for it.

The Queen

When we stayed with Nan and Bok, Nan had a habit of taking your plate while you were still eating and washing it up. Then she would start laying the table for the next meal. It's like she lived in a different time zone, always one meal ahead.

If I left a piece of Lego on the floor, or my differently abled Action Man, she would point an accusing finger at it and say, 'What if the Queen comes round for tea?'

She said this a lot. I began to be really scared of the Queen. The threat of one of her impromptu visits hovered over us constantly. I thought of her as a kind of guerrilla monarch with impossibly high standards of hygiene who would ambush you in your home without warning. What kind of person bursts into people's houses, runs a disapproving finger across their dusty shelves and then demands tea?

Sometimes when I had left my crayons out, I would lie in bed with my heart pounding, convinced I could hear the sound of horses' hooves and carriage wheels thundering up the cul-de-sac.

Wales

My first school trip was a week in Wales. It was the first time I'd spent the night away (apart from at Nan and Bok's) and I was pretty sure I would never make it home and live to see my eleventh birthday.

Twelve of us went to a very small cottage owned by a Welshman with a pony-tail and a beard. The boys slept on the floor in one bedroom and the girls slept on the floor in another bedroom. I felt sorry for our teacher because this meant she had to share a bedroom with the Welshman who owned the cottage.

In the day, the teacher and the man would tell us to go and look at the sheep and they would stay in their bedroom. In the evenings, he would play us songs on his guitar (often a couple of Father Christmas classics).

He didn't have much food in his cottage. We were very hungry. I came downstairs in the night to look for peanut butter and our teacher was sitting on the Welshman's lap. I was glad they were getting on so well.

One day, when we were bored of looking at sheep, they took us out for a walk. It was March and it was freezing. We walked to the top of a mountain and then the Welshman showed us how to 'ski' down it by running and throwing ourselves head first down the mountain. Our descent was stopped by a snowdrift. As my face ploughed into the snowdrift, I found myself peering over a sheer drop.

On the way back to the cottage, we got lost and ended up the wrong side of a fast-flowing river. The Welshman waded across and walked downstream. Then, one by one, we jumped into the stream, got washed down some rapids and, as we passed him, he would fish us out by our hoods. As we walked back to the cottage, our clothes stiffened into ice.

I was so homesick that week that it hurt. A sharp yearning that made me catch my breath. I didn't tell anyone I was homesick. Instead I wrote a lot of haikus about sheep.

Trophies

My brother didn't mind school trips. He went off happily without a backwards glance. To our amazement, he even won Tidiest Bedroom Trophy on one school trip. Although it turned out that this was because he hadn't opened his suitcase.

Don't relax

Granny was dangerous. She would swoop into rooms and give engulfing cuddles and wet kisses when you were least expecting it. She would teach us rude limericks and laugh and clap loudly when we were made to recite them. She would swear and lavish unwanted gifts on us – a ten-year-old Thai desk diary, a large rotting fur hat, a pair of men's braces. She would walk into the bathroom when you were on the loo. She had paintings of naked people on the walls. She smelt expensive and had a stash of crisp £1 notes that she would give you if you could guess the last digit of the serial number. She cooked delicious meals and while you were eating them would remind you that each peeled potato and each shelled pea was a minute of her life. She wanted to hear about gossip and scandal and calamity. If you had been to a wedding or a christening, she wanted only to hear about what had gone wrong. She asked about school but was only interested in who you didn't like and why.

She didn't answer the phone or the doorbell. She would gather everyone for lunch and then demand that nobody say anything interesting while she was out of the room. We would obediently exchange stilted small talk, terrified that she might come back and catch us being accidentally fascinating. Occasionally she would bark at my father: 'DON'T RELAX!' An unnecessary command as I have never seen him relax in his whole life.

Grandpa

I loved climbing the stairs to the very top of Granny and Grandpa's house. This is where Grandpa worked. Every day, he sat on a wooden chair with his legs crossed, a board on his lap, a pipe in his mouth, writing longhand with an ink pen. He had spent so many hours doing this, the chair had warped and become moulded to his shape.

I would sit opposite him, playing with pipe cleaners, enjoying the serenity as he wrote.

When he published a book of short stories, he would give me a copy and in exchange I would give him a copy of my latest (mainly budgie-related) stories which I had written in pencil in an exercise book. We would then critique each other's work.

Grandpa always had an amused smile on his face. I think he was amused by the people and the stories in his head. He was always a little distracted, hovering between this world and his fictional world, half listening out for a word or a phrase from one which he could use in the other.

Every afternoon, he would go out shopping. I always felt he was shopping for characters rather than groceries. We talked about writing. I thought that if you started writing one minute earlier or one minute later, the story would turn out completely differently (for the budgie) whereas he felt the story was there, waiting for you to excavate it.

I think it was in that room, bending pipe cleaners and listening to the sound of his pen on the paper and the more distant sounds of Granny slamming cupboards and swearing, that I learnt that writing could be a lifeline, an escape and a reason for getting up in the morning.

Living the dream

I wanted to mark the moment I became a woman. I decided the height of sophistication would be to eat alone in the Wimpy in Elephant and Castle shopping centre. That symbolic act would prove I had crossed the threshold from childhood into adulthood.

I saved my pocket money for weeks, and finally the day came. I walked to the shopping centre, had a browse in Woolworths, then I strolled into the Wimpy and asked for a table for one. I sat down and perused the menu, trying to look refined and debonair. I ordered a burger and a milkshake. I sat eating my burger and watching the cockroaches run up and down the wall. Life couldn't get better than this. I was living the dream.

I am woman, hear me suck the end of my strawberry milkshake through a straw – I wanted to roar.

Texas

Secondary school was a whole different ball game. You had to go in whether you felt like it or not. And you had to do lessons. And you had to wear a uniform. And you couldn't go home any time you wanted to. It was like prison.

I had friends – Susan, Swati, Big Trace – but I was miserable. I didn't like being in the playground. It was cold and noisy and scuffly. So I volunteered to be a Lab Monitor. This meant staying in the lab at break time and looking after the school animals. The lab stank of gas and farty-smelling chemicals and was also cold. But it was indoors and you were slightly less likely to get hit in the face by a football.

The school animals were gerbils, tadpoles and locusts. The tadpoles reduced drastically in number day by day, leaving one enormous tadpole called Texas ('The Big One', named after a carpet advert at the time). I didn't work out what Texas was up to at the time.

Meanwhile, the gerbils were constantly having babies despite the fact that I rigorously kept the boy gerbils and the girl gerbils apart (based on which ones looked like boys and which ones looked like girls). Then the babies kept wriggling through the bars of the cages. I would post them back, but as quickly as I did, they squirmed out again and rushed lemming-like towards the edge of the worktop.

The locusts were the most trouble. They stank. And they escaped ALL the time. Looking back, I realise that every single lesson of every day, kids probably took the lid off and let them have a little swarm around. But at the time, it was a complete mystery.

I spent most break times searching the lab on my hands and knees for locusts, hoping desperately that I wouldn't find one. They were very sticky and fluttery and jumpy and if I caught one and tried to put it back in the glass box, several more would escape in the process.

When I was down to my last locust, I was determined to find it. I searched the shelves of dusty jars of floating animal foetuses, I looked behind the yellowing textbooks, I opened every musty cupboard full of cracked petri dishes. Nothing.

I stood up. I turned to the skeleton hanging on a hook next to me. Something wasn't quite right. I looked again. Slowly. Carefully. And then I saw it. The locust was in the eye socket of the skeleton.

I screamed. And fainted.

That's when I learnt I'm not very good with responsibility.

The Witch

Mum is the jumpiest person I have ever known. Someone can drop a Malteser onto carpet several streets away and she will leap into the air with a piercing scream. This is all the more surprising as she has a sneeze so sudden and loud that I've witnessed bowels evacuate in its presence.

When left unsupervised, Mum buys nick-nacks. Her philosophy is that you can never have enough tiny jugs. The other thing she collects is wildly eccentric black hats, which is why we, as a family, refer to her as The Witch. She has one hat that crouches on her head, teetering and tilting like a drunk chimney; one that hovers like an angry cloud; one that perches, puckered and rumpled; one that squats, battered and gnarled; one that lurks, lumpen and crumpled – and one colourful one for special occasions that looks like it is roosting on her head.

She is impervious to people openly laughing at her as she walks down the street and no amount of begging, pleading or insulting can dissuade her from wearing them. These hats caused me endless suffering as a teenager, which, if anything, inspired her to buy more, bigger, weirder hats. Nothing makes her happier than other people's suffering. I have made her happy by tripping over the dog, fainting and once falling fully clothed into a swimming pool. But the happiest I have ever seen her was when my brother was chased by a furious horse. I think that was the best day of her life.

Robertson's Giant Limb

Susan had everything I wanted. Straight hair, a skateboard and scabies.

Once a year the nurse would arrive at school to give us a medical. She would check our hair for nits and weigh us and measure us. I desperately hoped she would find I was suffering from some exotic malady that would allow me to stay at home. I'd read about Robertson's Giant Limb in a textbook in the library and had been praying to God/ Jimmy Osmond that He would make my right leg grow ginormous. But the nurse found nothing. Not even a nit.

Sheep

At school there was a boy who had a shaky voice. Every time he spoke, the entire class would baa until what he was saying was drowned out. Sometimes the French teacher would join in. Sometimes the boy would join in, hoping that this gesture of goodwill would stop the bleating. It didn't.

Sometimes just the sight of him prompted bleating. He spent his entire childhood being followed down corridors to the echoes of noisy bleating. As soon as one child did it, the rest, like sheep, would follow.

Jelly

Swati was very thin. There was nothing for her to eat at school dinners. She couldn't eat meat. And she didn't like potatoes. All she ate was jelly. One day as she scraped her jelly from her bowl, I said, 'There's hoof in jelly.'

Swati said she didn't believe me. But I assured her that Nan had told me. And Nan was always right.

From then on Swati ate nothing at lunch time.

Woodwork

Our woodwork teacher had a bald head, a moustache and a Morris Minor Traveller with wood trimming. One day, some older boys came into the lab (while I was looking for locusts) and turned on all the gas taps and claimed the woodwork teacher had just 'sent off for a Thai Bride'. I felt sick. I wasn't sure if it was the gas or the Thai Bride.

They also claimed that the woodwork teacher hated spending money. They said if his wife was ill, he would come into chemistry lessons and try to make medicine for her by looking at the ingredients on a packet and finding the nearest equivalent chemicals.

I watched the woodwork teacher closely after this. He seemed to treat his car the same way he treated his wife. He didn't spend any money on it. And if it had a problem, he wouldn't take it to the garage.

Eventually, the car gave up on him. But he refused to pay the £20 for it to be picked up and taken to the scrap yard. So, using the woodwork tools from school, he started sawing the car into pieces. It took weeks. By the time he had finished, the tools were too blunt for us to make our pipe racks in our woodwork lessons.

To fool the bin men and avoid a fine, he smuggled the pieces of Morris Minor into bin bags and put them out with the rubbish over the course of several months.

I used to worry that if the bin men did check his rubbish, they might find pieces of Thai Bride too.

Adding up

Mr Mahmood was our maths teacher. He had a real passion for maths. I found maths bewildering but he understood everything. Nothing was beyond his comprehension. He loved maths. He found it beautiful. Astonishing. Magical. He would try to communicate this to us. But he spoke with an accent and every time he opened his mouth, he was met by a chorus of chicken noises. This appeared to be something to do with the fact that he was from Pakistan. The boy with the shaky voice always looked relieved when the sheep noises abated and the chicken noises started up.

After a while, Mr Mahmood developed a twitch. Much to the delight of the class. And sometimes, when the chicken noises reached a crescendo, he would have tears in his eyes.

I can picture him, chalk in hand, with a board full of equations behind him, staring at us in confusion. The first problem he couldn't solve.

Crime and punishment

Being invisible was a good skill to have at secondary school. If the boys noticed you, they would grab your bag and empty it out, hoping to find sanitary towels or tampons they could humiliate you with. If girls noticed you they would comment on your looks or clothes. If teachers noticed you, they would ask you a question and if you didn't know the answer, you'd be in trouble and if you did know the answer, you'd be in a different kind of trouble.

I wasn't very good at school. Partly because it was dangerous to be good at anything, but also because I mainly knew about haikus and buying cigarettes. Science came as a horrible shock. Nobody had warned me about its existence. French seemed ludicrous. Why speak another language badly when there were so many words in my own language that I still needed to learn? Maths was upsetting. It involved witnessing the emotional deterioration of Mr Mahmood. Writing was really all I had ever cared about. But when we had to write a story for homework, I was given detention. The teacher said I had plagiarised. This was one of the words in the English language that I was yet to understand. But when I looked it up, I was furious. I considered not bothering doing my homework, but I loved writing. So I wrote and I took the detentions and I spent the time carving the word 'plagiarism' into the desk.

Ian

One year, we couldn't afford to take Flo back to her roots, so instead The Witch arranged for us to house-sit for some friends of hers in the country. She was very excited because she said there were lots of animals for us to play with. It was only when we got there that we discovered the animals we could 'play' with were three stallions, eighteen mares, four foals, a ram called Raymond and sixteen ewes. It was a farm. Specifically, a working stud farm.

The owners were getting into their car as we arrived. They ordered us to throw the cats out every night so they could hunt for food and assured us something was bound to go wrong. 'Last time the cow got struck by lightning!' said the woman cheerfully.

I asked anxiously how the cow was. 'Delicious!' said the man. 'Nice smoky flavour.' And they left.

We went into the rather dilapidated house and discovered inside an uncountable number of cats and a couple of dogs. Flo was such an urban dog that she was out of her comfort zone surrounded by grass and fields and real animals. I felt sorry for her when, as she tucked into her bowl of Chum, the various cats and dogs rather pointedly brought in a whole parade of rabbits, voles, mice and birds that they had killed. Flo pretended not to notice. After dinner, she made a half-hearted attempt to chase a cat, more out of duty than pleasure, and spent the rest of the night under the table, nursing a scratched ear.

The next day we went out to survey our kingdom and to nervously count the animals and see whether the number was the same as the day before. There was loud, unnerving stamping and snorting coming from the restless stallions in the stables. And Raymond the Ram had become very interested in a rather loose bit of fence. We found a barn with a ping-pong table upstairs covered in bird shit. If you were clever, you could win by causing the ball to skid off the shit, making it unreturnable. If you were *really* skilled, you could angle it so that the ball AND the other player fell through the hole in the floor.

Best of all, there was a motorbike. It had no keys – you had to hotwire it to start it – and it had no brakes; you had to crash to stop. I spent the rest of the day roaring loudly up and down the lane, passing a blur of horses and slaloming round some ewes who had found the gap in the fence and were wondering what to do next.

Later the phone rang. The Patriarchy answered. 'Just calling to check on the snake situation?' said the voice.

'What snake situation?' asked The Patriarchy, as nonchalantly as he could while tucking his trousers into his socks. For the rest of the day we walked with very high knees.

I soon discovered that one of the dogs, a retriever called Ian, was my soulmate. He had really taken the description 'retriever' to heart and spent the day bestowing various unasked-for gifts upon you. Socks, shoes, vegetables, stones, soap, branches, toothbrushes, daffodils, anything you could ever want and more. Much, much more.

One day he came back with something that looked alarmingly like a rotting leg. We rushed out to count the animals again and also to count the legs on the animals.

That night there was a power cut. We found a candle and played Snap in the dark. When it was bedtime, we obediently attempted to throw the cats outside. My brother saw something move and grabbed it only to discover it was his foot. It was no good, we couldn't find them. We discovered later that they had given themselves the night off and eaten Flo's food and every single piece of food in the house.

The next day it was time for sex. Tracey, the stable girl, went and got one of the stallions, who rampaged wild-eyed towards the field full of mares.

'Think!' shouted Tracey to the stallion. 'Concentrate!' she bellowed as it stamped and snorted and reared and lunged at the mare. I went off for a thoughtful hurtle on the motorbike, but as I rounded a corner, a green monster staggered in front of me. I swerved sharply and crashed into some nettles. On inspection, the green monster was Flo, who had fallen into an unexpected pond. She absolutely stank. We limped back to the house together. The other animals rushed to see what the interesting smell was and finally looked at Flo with something approaching respect.

The final night, surrounded by the now completely domesticated and overweight cats, we heard a roll of thunder. I did not like storms and neither, it seemed, did Ian. We spent the night together, Ian and me, in my bed, surrounded by shoes, potatoes, a spoon, several dusters, a spanner, a cauliflower, a tin opener, an oven glove, a toilet brush, a kiwi and anything else Ian could lay his paws on. And it helped. Together we weathered the storm.

Woman

My first boyfriend was called Alan. We met at drama club. He asked if he could walk me home. I said we could just get the bus, but he insisted on walking me. All the way from Deptford to Elephant and Castle. After that, we seemed to be boyfriend and girlfriend.

He was very romantic but he would stop holding my hand when we were walking on busy streets. I asked him why and he said he would show me. We walked hand in hand and over the course of five minutes, we were spat at, sworn at, and various people accused Alan of coming over here and taking our jobs and our women. I was secretly very excited to be called a woman.

The surprise

When I was fifteen, I suddenly found myself involved in an inhumane social experiment commonly known as a French Exchange. I thought this was a Very Bad Idea. But then I thought most things that involved leaving the house were a Very Bad Idea. My parents said that if things got really terrible, I should contact them and say 'Plan B' down the phone. They then clarified that things such as different pillows didn't count as really terrible.

I arrived in France and was picked up by the French Father. We established on the journey to his house that when Actual French people spoke Actual French at the Actual Speed that Actual French people speak Actual French, I couldn't understand a word. I was beginning to feel panicky. Maybe I could just hide in my bedroom in the chic apartment that he almost certainly lived in. But he pointed his car away from the chic apartments and up an Alp.

After a lot of wiggly windy roads, we arrived at a sort of barn without a proper roof. My look of horror was surpassed by his fourteen-year-old daughter's look of horror. She hadn't known I was coming. I was a surprise. And clearly, I wasn't a nice surprise.

The Mother showed me round the barn. There was a bunk bed. Their seven-year-old son and his friend were sharing the bottom bunk, and their daughter and I would share the top bunk. There was a space with an old filthy oven and a table – which was covered in cats and dogs eating from the plates which had our lunch on. Outside there was a hole in the ground instead of a loo. No bath, no shower. I was in hell.

As I unpacked Anxious Bear, the fourteen-year-old daughter explained, between puffs on her Gauloise, that she was having an affair with a married man and he had rented the house further down the Alp so they could see each other. My job was to make myself scarce and say nothing so as not to ruin her fun. This I could do. My main skillset was making myself scarce and saying nothing.

At night, I would lie in the top bunk, wearing all my clothes because it was FREEZING, staring at the stars through the non-existent roof and wondering how I could escape. How long would it take me to get down an Alp in the dark? And then what would I do? And would I get lost and die of hypothermia? I was pretty sure I was dying of hypothermia anyway.

There were no phones, there was no post office, there was no Ian to comfort me and there was no way of communicating the words 'Plan B' to my parents. I silently screamed 'Plan B' at the moon, but it ignored me.

Then one day, the Father gathered us together and we got in the car, everyone except me and the seven-year-olds smoking furiously. We went to visit an Elderly Relative in a nearby town. And she had a phone. I pointed at the phone in as French a way as possible and then at myself, saying, '*Moi?*' The Elderly Relative was not at all keen. There was intense French discussion. Then the Father nodded and said, '*Une minute.*' I dialled the number for The Patriarchy and The Witch. As soon as they heard my voice, they started to tell me about Flo's latest phantom pregnancy and which of my toys was currently being suckled. I whispered, 'Plan B!' urgently at them.

'Hmm? What?'

'Plan B!'

'What's Plan B?'

'You know! Plan B!'

'She said something about Plan B . . .'

'It's the code!' I hissed, exasperated.

'She said it's a code . . .'

'Plan B! Plan B!' I shouted.

The phone went dead. The Elderly Relative had cut me off.

A few days later, I was packing Anxious Bear back into my bag. Once the fourteen-year-old slipped out to be with her lover that night, I would make my escape. I would walk down the Alp in the dark and try to find civilisation. But just then, a post office van drove up to the barn. A postman got out and delivered a telegram to the Father. The Father read the telegram and looked at me solemnly.

'Your grandmother is very ill. You must return home.'

'YES!' I said, punching the air. They looked shocked. 'I've never liked her,' I explained.

That's when I discovered I was a terrible liar.

The house

One January morning, as I walked to school in Deptford from New Cross station, I saw that a house, almost opposite the school, was burnt out. The windows gaped, black streaks escaping from their horrified mouths.

When I got into school, I found out that Yvonne, who was sixteen, had died in the fire, along with twelve friends. Some had burnt to death, some had been overcome by smoke, others had thrown themselves out of windows and landed on the railings. Yvonne had been having a party for her birthday.

There was talk amongst the pupils that it had been a racist attack. But the police and the media suggested that black youths had started the fire because they hadn't been allowed in.

I kept imagining Yvonne and her friends dying in the house or on the pavement outside.

Every day, I passed the house. Day after day. Week after week. Year after year. The carcass of the house remained the same. The unmarked tomb stood, full of ashes. A reminder of what had been forgotten. Of who had been forgotten. Nobody ever found out what happened that night.

After thirty years, a small blue plaque was placed on the renovated building.

Names

Susan's name wasn't really Susan. And her surname wasn't really her surname either. She had arrived in England with her parents and her seven brothers and one sister. She told me the immigration officer taking their names in England couldn't understand what they were saying so he just wrote down names that he knew.

Susan's name was really Bo San. Bo means 'she who questions' in Chinese and describes an intelligent but humble person who is intuitive, kind and patient.

The immigration officer who gave Bo her new name was obviously an older man because he gave all these young Chinese children the names of older white people. So Susan's brothers were called Len, Ken, Tony, Brian, etc. I expect the meaning of these names is that they were people he knew down the British Legion.

Growing pains

By the time I was sixteen, I was buying a lot of pregnancy tests. Not for myself, for my friend Karen, who constantly thought she was pregnant, despite the fact that she had never had sex.

'I heard they can jump!' she explained while we stood in the queue to pay for yet another test.

When the test came back negative she would say, 'Well, I'm staggerblasted.' It was a staggerblasting time.

Ali was in trouble because she kept sneaking out of her house at night and sitting on the maths teacher's lawn. Eileen was sleeping with the science teacher and the rest of us took it in turns keeping guard while they had sex in the classroom.

Nina and Sharon had abortions on the same day. Lee's brother killed himself. Life seemed to be spiralling out of control.

My friend Marilyn was different. She seemed to have everything under control. She was 'shooby', which was a word she used a lot and which, sadly, I was not shooby enough to understand. Things just worked out for her. I loved hanging out with her. She plucked her eyebrows, she knew all the words to *The Rocky Horror Picture Show* and her biggest problem was which shoes she should wear to her sister's wedding.

In the summer, we decided we should go travelling. We arranged to meet in Paris on a certain day but forgot to say where or when. So I just started wandering round the streets and I bumped into her. You see? Things always worked out when Marilyn was involved. We met up with more friends and went Interrailing round Italy. We decided to save money by not eating and not staying at any hotels. We became so exhausted and malnourished that we would instantly fall asleep when we sat down. I have slept on benches near all the major sights of Italy, while insects feasted on my crispy skin. I think most of me is in a mosquito somewhere in Venice.

Meanwhile, Marilyn left early to go to her sister's wedding. She still hadn't worked out which shoes to wear.

Port

Sarah was unhappy. She kept raiding her parents' drinks cupboard. As a cry for help, this was a bad choice because her parents didn't drink so she had to make her way through a lot of very old sherry and port before they noticed.

I remember staying the night with her when her parents were away. We swigged down sherry and talked. We turned on the television and saw that a passenger ferry had sunk outside Zeebrugge. I remember she cried but I felt nothing. I don't know why, it just seemed so unreal, looking at a ship lying on its side in the sea. I didn't really believe it could have happened.

The next day, when I went to school with a sherry hangover, I discovered Marilyn's sister and her new husband had been on the ferry. They found their bodies six weeks later.

Rite of passage

Suddenly adulthood. Suddenly I was that budgie who had fallen out of the nest. And I had no clue what to do. Except I was pretty sure it involved RESPONSIBILITY, and that is a big word for a budgie.

One way of knowing you have crossed from girlhood to womanhood is that men stop furtively masturbating at you from bushes and start shouting things at you from cars. It's a beautiful moment. There should be some kind of ceremony.

Smiling

Another way I knew I had grown up is that when I was
at school, the teachers used to shout, 'Pritchett! Wipe
that smile off your face!' and when I became an adult,
strangers would pass me in the street and shout, 'Try
smiling!'

ABC

I'm not a procrastinator. If anything, I like to get things done early. I had a mid-life crisis at seventeen, failed all my exams and ended up living in a bedsit for a year while I tried to work out what to do with my life. Eventually I applied to do teacher training at Birmingham Polytechnic. It was a terrible idea, but I couldn't think of a better one.

I got lodgings in a house near the polytechnic. The landlady was a woman called Pat with a thick Black Country accent. The house was huge and in the process of being refurbished. The walls were stripped back to the plaster, there was no heating and very little furniture. It was absolutely freezing. My room contained just a bed with a thin white duvet lying on top, which looked like a layer of snow.

Pat had a husband (who she threatened constantly with divorce), three children and a whole host of lodgers. Her favourite lodgers were ballet dancers because they didn't eat much. One ballet dancer, Alice, had an unusually healthy appetite. Pat asked for a ticket to see her perform. When Alice returned home that night, Pat told her she'd enjoyed the show but was surprised how fat Alice looked on stage. Problem solved.

Pat's other favourite lodgers were train drivers. They didn't stay long and because of the shift system she could sometimes have them hot-bunking – six train drivers sleeping in three beds in swift rotation.

It wasn't unusual for me to come home from college and find she had rented my room out to someone else and I would have to sleep on the floor of her children's bedroom or, one time, in the corridor. Because I was training to be a teacher, she asked me to give some extra lessons to the children. The children were her least favourite lodgers because they didn't pay AND they ate a lot.

I sat down with her seven-year-old daughter and tried to help with her spelling. She was really struggling. I gave her a clue.

'It's the letter that comes after C,' I said.

'What do you mean?'

'You know, A, B, C . . .' I paused and looked at her meaningfully.

'What do you mean?'

'The alphabet,' I said. 'Shall we sing it together?'

'What's the alphabet?' she asked, confused.

'You know,' I said encouragingly, 'there are twenty-six letters . . .'

'Twenty-six??' she wailed, horrified.

'Yes,' I said. 'And they all come in a certain order . . .'

As I cheerily launched into a loud rendition of the ABC (pretty much all I had learnt to do on my course), the colour drained from her face. Why did everything have to be so complicated? Why did everything have to be so difficult? Why was everything so confusing? I knew exactly how she felt.

The Word of God

When I went to college, I got in with the wrong crowd. Christians. I had been raised an atheist but I had occasional lapses in my atheism where I doubted the non-existence of God. Also, I liked that they had an answer to everything. And although I didn't believe, I found their convictions very comforting.

One day, a girl called Eve invited me to go with her and her friends to visit people's houses and tell them about Jesus. I was worried about this as I still thought of God as Jimmy Osmond in a sheet.

One woman opened her door and said that she had been a non-believer all her life but then last week, a miracle had happened and God had spoken to her.

'What happened?' asked the Christians eagerly.

'There was a fire in my flat and I was fast asleep and I suddenly heard this booming voice,' said the woman. 'It was God calling to me.'

'What did He say?' asked the Christians excitedly.

'He said, "GET THE FUCK OUT OF BED!"'

Now that was a God I could believe in.

Bump

One of my friends at college, Francesca, was everything I wanted to be. She had straight hair, she read poetry, she spoke other languages, she had a boyfriend who could drive and she knew what she wanted to do with her life. She really had her shit together.

One weekend, we went to Pizza Hut. As students this was a favourite. You'd go to the all-you-can-eat buffet and pile food so high it was leaning against your arm, and then you'd cram as much as possible into your body and live off it for days.

As I returned to the table with my tower of cold sweetcorn and grated carrot, I noticed that Francesca only had a few croutons on her plate. She told me she wasn't feeling well. She felt sick. I presumed she was hungover, which was how I felt most of the time, but she said no, she was pregnant.

She couldn't tell her parents (they were Christians) and she couldn't tell her tutors (because she was worried she'd be chucked off her course – or they would tell her parents) so she had decided that the best course of action was to just pretend that she wasn't pregnant.

Over the next few months, by sheer willpower, she managed to not look pregnant. She carried on with her course. She told nobody.

As the summer holidays approached, she told me she was planning to go to Glastonbury.

'But isn't that the exact date when . . . ?' I started to say.

'No, no. That isn't happening.'

I looked at the bump now finally beginning to show under her long baggy shirt. I was pretty sure it was happening.

At Glastonbury, in a tent, in the rain, she went into labour. She called me, furious, from the hospital. I went to see her the next day. She looked exhausted and defeated. Nurses kept coming in to weigh the baby or help with feeding, only to be told the baby was next door, she wasn't keeping it. Francesca couldn't even bear to look at her. This was not part of the plan for her life. And she was terrified her parents might find out.

I went next door, where Francesca's boyfriend's parents were holding the baby and sobbing. They asked me to take photos of them with their granddaughter before she was taken away. They said she was going to a foster mum's the next day and six weeks later she would be adopted for good.

Back at college in September, I visited Francesca in her digs, a tiny attic room at the top of a house. She talked about the bands at Glastonbury, about her course, about getting a student loan, but about nothing else.

I couldn't stop worrying about her daughter, about what would become of her, about how she would never know Francesca or the details of her birth. Maybe I should adopt her? Could I adopt her? I should definitely adopt her. But no, apparently troubled penniless nineteen-year-olds are not considered suitable adoptive parents.

On the very final day of the six weeks, Francesca called. She was going to go and get her baby. Her boyfriend was going to drive her to the foster mum's and she was going to pick her daughter up. Then the next day, he was going to drive her home and she was going to tell her parents.

Exuding

My teacher training wasn't going very well. On my first day at a primary school, I was asked to take the six-year-old girls swimming. I rounded them up and ran to the pool, snaking in and out of traffic, forgetting I had thirty small girls scuttling after me. Once we got to the pool, I discovered only two of the thirty girls would be swimming, all the others being Muslim and forbidden to take their clothes off. I sat on the side with the twenty-eight non-swimming girls, who told me solemnly that the two girls who were swimming would be thrown into the fiery lake of fire for their sins. These six-year-olds seemed so sure, so confident in their beliefs. I envied them their faith, though not their fiery lake of fire.

Back at school, I was put on playground duty. I tried to stalk round the playground exuding authority, but I've never been good at exuding. After a few minutes, a girl approached me and asked me if I was new. I said I was.

'Are you lonely?' she asked.

'No, I'm busy,' I answered curtly.

'You can be my friend if you haven't got any other friends,' she told me.

I tried to explain that I wasn't a pupil, I was a teacher.

'You're not a teacher!' she laughed.

The next day I dropped out of the course.

This six-year-old girl knew me better than I knew myself. I wasn't a teacher and I was really lonely.

A cockroach in my gusset

After dropping out of college, I wasn't sure what to do
with myself. The Patriarchy suggested I go to stay with a
family he knew in America and help out while I thought
about what to do next. This seemed like a terrible idea.
My other experiences of travelling (French Exchange
and Interrailing round Europe) had really narrowed
my horizons and I was pretty keen to stay within my
postcode. But I had no money and nowhere to stay and
nobody was finding my 'different pillows' argument very
compelling.

We rehearsed a new and improved version of the Plan B
plan and I packed my clothes in a borrowed suitcase that I
discovered separated from the handle after every step.

Once I arrived, I didn't take my coat off for several
days. I wasn't prepared for how *foreign* America was. But
the family was wonderful, the two-year-old girl was very
maternal towards me and the baby was glorious. If I just
stayed in the house, I would probably be fine.

'We're going travelling!' the parents announced a few
days later.

A wave of icy fear swept up and down my body and
eventually made a nest in my stomach.

'Would you like to borrow a different suitcase?' they asked.

I nodded. My eyes drifted to the phone. Was it too soon to make the Plan B phone call? I hadn't taken my coat off yet . . .

A few days later, I found myself in a Winnebago. A mobile torture chamber that did not have a proper loo or a proper shower or any kind of bath.

This was a fearless family. They would do anything and, far from a phone or any means of Plan B-ing the situation, I got swept up in their enthusiasm. We went to the desert. We flew down the Grand Canyon in a glass-bottomed helicopter, we went white-water rafting, we went to the Petrified Forest (much of which I found in the two-year-old's nappy later). We went to the mountains. We marvelled at how they had opened a coffee shop in Seattle where all you could buy was coffee and decided it would never catch on.

Everything was different. I felt alive. I was noticing things I'd never noticed before. As I got dressed one morning, I realised I'd previously never noticed how heavy my knickers were. I looked down and there was an enormous cockroach in my gusset. I threw the knickers out of the door as far as I could. Beware weighty underwear.

After that we went to the East Coast. We travelled through New England and abandoned our Winnebago to get on a tiny wobbly boat to a tiny island in Maine. It was like being Robinson Crusoe but with slightly fewer cannibals.

In the daytime, we sat and had meals in one main

log cabin, we caught fish on the shore and we explored the island (which took about five minutes). At night, we slept in little individual log cabins dotted around the woods. There were frequent power cuts as the electricity was provided by a generator and we were regularly plunged into darkness. Then we would have to feel our way through the pitch blackness to our cabins and crawl into our sleeping bags. This was terrifying. I stumbled through the woods, arms outstretched, wondering what monsters I was blindly blundering towards. Only the sound of distant laughter from the family (who thought it was great fun) helped guide me to my cabin. Then I lay, not sure if my eyes were open or closed, imagining what else might be in my cabin with me. I mean, obviously a shitload of spiders. Maybe a resentful cockroach who had tracked me down. And possibly some of those long creepy-crawlies with zillions of legs. Or those other ones with waggly wavy feeler things instead of eyes. I couldn't sleep. It was time to make the phone call.

The next day, in the main log cabin, I asked nonchalantly if there was a phone. There *was* a phone. It was a wind-up phone with a very particular foible. It would only keep the connection if a man was speaking to another man. I'd never heard of a sexist phone before, but the father said he'd demonstrate. He was arranging the next leg of our journey and had to make a phone call. He wound up the phone and dialled and started doing a passable impression of Barry White. But every time his voice went up, when asking a question or sounding incredulous, the line went dead.

I realised I didn't have the vocal range to make my Plan B call. I was stuck.

By the time we got off the island, back to civilisation and telephones that were more modern in their attitudes, the feeling had passed. And as we made our way back to Georgetown, it was Plan A all the way.

My calling

Back at home, I had to get a job. I had to persuade someone to pay me money to do something. But what could I do? Apparently wanting to spend twenty-three hours a day wearing pyjamas is not a vocation. And wanting to eat my own body weight in Wagon Wheels is not a calling.

But there was a job that would allow me to do both those things . . . AND monetise the fact that I spent a lot of time sitting around watching TV.

Writing.

Scandinavia

Having decided I was a writer, my first job involved writing precisely one word. My name. On a sticker. I got a job at Catford Broadway Theatre as an usher for an Irish Jig competition. Lots of tiny children had come from all over the world to compete. I was fascinated by the way their faces stayed so still and so solemn while their legs went bananas. My face stayed still and calm while my brain went bananas.

The competition was furiously fought. The Scandinavians won in every category. I turned to my fellow usher, who was older than me and seemed to know everything.

'I wonder why the Scandinavians are so good at Irish dancing?' I said.

'There's not much else to do in Scandinavia but dance,' she said, sagely.

I wished I could be as worldly as she was.

Fizzy pâté

My next job was at Harrods. I worked at the charcuterie
counter. I sold cured meats which had to be sliced in
a huge slicer. I never got the hang of this and cut my
fingertips off pretty much every time I used it. The good
news is, when I turn to a life of crime, I'm going to be very
hard to catch.

I also sold weird curled gnarled dried meats that were
very expensive and smelt of the fart you would later be
doing. And I sold lots and lots of pâté. I would come home
with my pockets stuffed with pâté. There are two things I
would say about this, with the benefit of hindsight. One,
stealing is wrong. Two, never eat fizzy pâté that has been
in your pocket all day.

The most popular items I sold at my counter were
truffles and caviar. It's an odd situation when the change
you are giving your customers is more than your week's
wages. One man came and asked how much our biggest
truffle cost. I told him it was £500. He paid the money,
took the lid off the jar, picked the truffle out and stood
there eating it like an apple.

At Christmas, we had a different type of customer.
Not the truffle-eating types, the wild-eyed panic-stricken
customers looking for the perfect gift.

One Christmas, a middle-aged man was the first through the doors. He set off like a hare being chased by dogs, rushing round the shop. He was on a mission. He had to find the perfect present. I saw him again at lunchtime, sprinting past the smoked salmon counter, looking even more alarmed. Clearly a lot was riding on this gift.

As the store was closing and I was counting the money in my till, I noticed a hunched figure shuffling towards me. It was him. Staring at the ground, he held something out to me. A tea towel. I took his money and put the tea towel in a bag. He'd blown it. And we both knew.

Making a living

Very early on in my career I started to 'make a living'.
This was because a vending machine near where I lived
was faulty. I would go to buy a Marathon and put in 50p
and it would give me £1 change. This machine quickly
became my main source of income. And of food. When it
was finally fixed, I had to move in with my brother.

George

I enjoyed my time in Catford and in charcuterie, but I
wanted to find something more writey. I'm a wordsmith,
as you can tell. Then I heard about a show called
Weekending on Radio 4. They accepted unsolicited
material and held an open meeting once a week. People
could just wander in off the street – and they did. A
collection of humans – some young hopefuls, some misfits,
some older angry people whose lives hadn't worked out
the way they'd planned and some people who just needed
somewhere to keep warm – gathered in a small hot room
in the corner of the BBC.

A producer would come in and discuss the stories
that they might be covering that week and then you
had twenty-four hours to come up with a joke or a
sketch, type it up and bring it back. Or post it in. There
were two typewriters in the room and a queue formed
for them immediately. Far too anxious to write under
pressure from an impatient queue, I went home and
tried to write there. If you got a joke or one-liner used,
you were paid £8. If a whole sketch was used, you were
paid £21 per minute. If your sketch lasted a minute
and a second, you were paid £42 (for entering a second
minute). The dream.

From then on, I spent Fridays shivering in my
brother's 2CV (the only place we had a radio) at 11 p.m.
with a stopwatch. I had to get in the passenger side and
scramble across to the driver's seat because the driver's
door was dented and stuck closed from where someone

had run into the car. And when I say run into, I mean it was a jogger who wasn't looking where he was going.

I remember the triumph I felt, sitting in the dark in the dented 2CV, hearing the first joke they used and punching the air with joy.

And then listening as my name on the credits was given as George. Of course it was. I was the only woman in the room. But that would change, wouldn't it? No. It wouldn't. It was twenty-five years later (and in a different country) when I finally got to write with other women.

Lassie

When my brother moved, I stayed with various friends.
I would move on after a few days so as not to outstay my
welcome. Much like Lassie. But without saving anyone
from a mineshaft.

I sometimes stayed with a friend at the top of a tall
tower block. Her dad was an Armenian businessman
and he would often return from business trips with tins
and tins of caviar which he gave to us. He didn't seem to
understand that we lived on a diet that consisted solely
of Kentucky Fried Chicken and banana-flavoured Angel
Delight. We didn't know what to do with the caviar, so
we gave it to the cat. The cat didn't like it either. It just
left it in the bowl. When friends came round, it seemed
very decadent that the cat's bowl was piled with uneaten
caviar.

Snails

Staying at other people's houses sometimes presented a bigger problem than different pillows. One house had dry rot, wet rot, mould, spores and a mouse 'situation'. One morning, as I was making myself breakfast, I wondered what the strange smell was. My question was answered when my toast popped out of the toaster and, simultaneously, a flaming mouse was catapulted out of the other side. It was both spectacular and deeply upsetting.

Another of the places I stayed in was infested with snails. I was scared of snails so when I slept on the floor, I used to draw a line of salt around my whole body. It looked like the chalk outline of a murder victim. But it worked. I woke up one morning and my friend discovered a snail trail going across her pillow, then a gap where her head had been, and then the snail trail resuming. I felt it would have been worse if the snail trail *hadn't* resumed after the gap. I also felt it was time to find my own place.

Cup of sugar

To my surprise, I managed to find a flat to rent quite
easily. It was in a small house near Peckham Rye which
had been divided in a somewhat haphazard way into
three flats. My flat had weird-shaped rooms at angles,
a lot of stairs and the kitchen was in a cupboard. The
bathroom, which was minuscule, was down several floors
and then back up several floors. The bath was about three
feet long – essentially a big sink on the floor. There were
also some really interesting stains on the carpet – one
looked like Bob Marley, another like Basil Brush, and
one near the front door was like a squirrel carrying a
handbag. Best of all, the rent was REALLY low.

Mine was the top flat, which was C, and the bottom
flat was A. This counter-intuitive system meant that
my doorbell often rang and I would answer the door to
various confused men who would look at me and say,
'No thank you,' and walk quickly away. I tried to be
neighbourly – 'If there's ever anything I can do . . .' I said.
'Cup of sugar . . . ?' I offered (I didn't have one, but I'd
heard people say that). The bell would ring at all times
of the day and night. It was utterly bewildering until
Donna, from Flat B, explained that Flat A was a brothel.
The men ringing my doorbell had not been interested in
trying whatever 'cup of sugar' was a euphemism for. I
was grateful and insulted that these men had not been
attracted to a puny woman in novelty slippers and a
beanie, but it made me wonder if I should try to find
someone who was.

Ferret

The problem was, the way I looked was not the way women in magazines look. I have the shoulders of a muppet. My freakishly long torso coupled with my unusually short legs makes me look like an eel is taking a ride on a gerbil. The overall effect is more ferret than human.

I was bald for years as a child and when, finally, some scratty hair started to form a thin, brush-like covering on my head, it stopped too soon. I'm all forehead. And for as long as I can remember, my brow has been furrowed. There's room for a lot of furrow.

My hair is curly. I have no say in what it decides to do. My choices are big hair or small hair.

All this is set off by a flat face, a snaggle-toothed smile and thin lips.

To make things worse, I'm told I dress like someone whose best clothes are in the wash.

I had always imagined that as I emerged into adulthood, my hair would straighten, my legs and fingernails would lengthen, I would develop fashion sense and I would be able to snap my fingers three times in that way that all the cool people do. Nope.

Spitting Image

After a couple of years on *Weekending*, I graduated to
Spitting Image. *Spitting Image* was a puppet show for
adults, featuring caricatures of politicians and celebrities.
It was created by Roger Law, who was more caricature
than human himself – just an angry beard with bloodshot
eyes who communicated only in swear words.

Sometimes I went to the puppet storeroom for
inspiration. Walking round the storeroom always made
me anxious. Shelves and shelves of politicians' heads
and torsos lying around, slowly rotting. The smell of
decomposing rubber was overwhelming. It was all a little
too symbolic.

The show was made all over the world and occasionally groups of people turned up to learn how to make the show in their country. It was unnerving to see a slightly South American version of yourself or a Dutch version of yourself. One time a group of Russians visited to see how the process worked. We explained that it was more complicated than you would think – artists drew caricatures of the politician or celebrity, then sculptors made clay busts from the caricatures, then foam moulds were created from the busts, then rubber was poured into the moulds and then finally the rubber was painted. It was an expensive and time-consuming procedure. Once a puppet had been created and dressed, it took a team of people to bring it to life. Several puppeteers per puppet (for hands, head, mouth, eye movement), a voice artist, writers, etc. The Russians had a very limited budget but seemed unfazed by this. Unlike other visitors, they took no photos, took no notes, recorded nothing. After they left, we found out why. They stole most of our puppets.

Spirit Muppet

Fozzie Bear is my Spirit Muppet. And like Fozzie, I have had my own Statler and Waldorf heckling me throughout my career. At first it was a little intimidating, but after a while I became strangely fond of the critics that I kept enraging.

When I first got a job on *Spitting Image*, they observed: 'What on earth went wrong? From its start in 1984 through to 1993 this was the best satire series on TV, but when the new team took over in 1994 things went from bad to worse. The whole thing adopted a very downmarket, tacky feel to it. The older *Spitting Image* series are unmissable – hilarious, well made, well thought-out. But the new guard ought to be ashamed for running this great series into the ground.'

The problem is, that only spurred me on.

Flirting vs squirting

I've never understood flirting. How do you know when it's happening? How do you know how to do it? How do you know whether you are doing it or not?

A man I liked once told me I looked like Robert Plant. Is that flirting? Another one told me if I grew a beard and wore a ruff, I'd look like Shakespeare. Did that count as being chatted up? Someone else told me Georgia was their favourite font. Hard to take credit for that. But thanks.

At a party once, I decided to give flirting a go. I asked a man what he was doing afterwards. He said, 'I'm going to go home, lift some weights, then I'll probably throw up, then lift some more weights, have a protein drink, lift more weights and throw up again.'

'Why do you keep throwing up?' I asked, horrified, backing away.

'Because when you're really pumping iron, you get such a rush of testosterone, it makes you throw up.'

It suddenly dawned on me that this might be flirting. I liked him, so I decided to flirt back.

'Yeah, I'll probably go home and do some needlepoint and then I'll get such a rush of oestrogen, I'll vomit over my cross-stitch.'

He left.

That's when I realised I should have been a badger. Badgers just go around secreting pheromones. I bet I'd be good at secreting. Or maybe I should have been a giraffe, and then I could just do a special wee. I'm really good at weeing. Or if I were a fish I could just go and squirt my eggs under a rock and wait for a male fish to hover over them. I'd be a great squirter.

Da diddly qua qua

My first relationships included an anorexic Adam Ant fan whose bones were sharp under his Hussars military jacket, a gay Italian who didn't feel he could come out after his brother had, a young man whose life had been changed after meeting the Nolans and who drove me around in his yellow Capri with a Nolans sun visor, a gorgeous man who called himself 'Paki' because that's what his friends called him, a black man whose family disapproved of him dating a white woman, a black man whose family wanted him to *only* date white women, and a man whose name was Itchy Alan (and who was allergic to his own dandruff).

I discovered that if you're a shy woman who doesn't say much but smiles a lot, people project onto you who they think you are or who they want you to be. This makes going on dates doubly interesting/terrifying. I would not only be finding out who they were, I would be finding out who they had decided I was. And the problem was, however much I did or didn't like *them*, I never liked their version of me.

Impressions

After *Spitting Image*, I wrote for a series of comedians and comedy shows. The first one I wrote for was *The Real McCoy*, described as a 'black sketch show'. I am not black, but I was told being a woman was close enough. It was 'another minority'.

After that I moved on to *Have I Got News for You*, Smith and Jones, Graham Norton and Rory Bremner. Writing for Rory Bremner was interesting. Watching him slip seamlessly from an impression of John Major to Tony Blair to Barry Norman was remarkable. His impressions of them seemed much more convincing than my impressions of Woman Who Knows What She Is Doing, Sane Woman, Girlfriend, Woman Not Crippled By Anxiety – or indeed Writer. The handy thing is, I didn't have to bother with imposter syndrome because as a woman who didn't go to Oxford or Cambridge, I *was* treated like an imposter.

Breaking up is hard to do

I had been going out with someone for a while and wanted to break up with him. But I didn't know how to do it. I finally mustered the courage and told him I didn't want to go out with him any more. He thought for a while and then said, 'Well, you don't want to go out with me, but I do want to go out with you, so one of us is going to be unhappy, so we might as well carry on as we are.'

That seemed like a watertight argument to me. We carried on seeing each other for another year.

Antichrist

My best friend Eve had moved round the corner from me. We spent hours hanging out, laughing, talking about nothing, talking about everything. We talked about all our different anxieties – finally I could be honest with someone. The only thing we didn't talk about was the fact that she was clearly gay. It just seemed like a no-go area.

One evening, after I'd drunk too many Southern Comfort and lemonades, we ended up kissing. This was a surprise on many counts. I'd never thought about it before, and it turned out she was the only person who hadn't realised she was gay.

She had wondered if she was once, but her mum had told her she absolutely definitely wasn't and that it was just a thyroid problem.

Eve begged me not to tell anyone but asked me if she could talk to someone at the church she went to about what had happened. I said she could if she wanted to.

I was in the kitchen when they arrived. Eve and a large group of people from the church. They removed any belongings she had left at my flat and then collected her clothes from the house she shared and took her to a new house, owned by the church. Eve called me later and told me, in a whispered conversation, that there was a woman there called Liz who was curing gay people with prayer.

She also said that the church wanted to exorcise me, but that didn't sound like much fun, so I said no. Then Eve said that Liz wanted to pray for me. I didn't really fancy that either, but Eve begged me to agree.

I went round to Liz's house, where there were several gay men and gay women living. She was marrying one of the gay men off to one of the gay women. This seemed like a terrible idea.

Liz invited me into her room and put her hand on my shoulder. She started telling me that two naked women's bodies together was sinful. Couldn't I see how wrong a naked woman with another naked woman was? If a woman was naked and then she lay down with another woman who was also naked, they would both be naked, together, lying nakedly, next to each other, all naked. As she spoke, her hand started stroking me and then moving lower.

I grabbed her hand and said I'd changed my mind. Then I ran like the clappers. This seemed like a lot of fuss about a Southern Comfort-fuelled kiss.

That night, I waited for Eve to come over, which she did. She came to tell me that Liz had said I was banned from crossing the threshold of any church ever and banned from crossing the threshold of the house of any Christian. Liz had also decided Eve must never see me again.

I'd spent a lot of time worrying I was the Messiah, but I hadn't thought to worry I might be the Antichrist. I lost my best friend and I couldn't tell anyone why because of my promise.

After this I decided to focus on my writing and not cross any more thresholds.

Peeping

Writing is the perfect job for an anxious person. You get
to do most of it at home in your pyjamas. It is utterly
anonymous. Nobody knows what writers look like.
Nobody knows their names. Other people literally talk on
your behalf. You get to peep out at the world between the
lines you've written.

Every so often you have to get dressed and go out
of the house and have a meeting which involves social
interaction. Nightmare. But these are usually as short as
they are pointless and soon you can scurry back to your
duvet and hide again.

Etc.

When I worked on shows with other writers, I was always the only woman in the room. But I often felt like I wasn't there at all. When I was working on a show with five other writers, we would sometimes get faxes with notes on the script. The faxes would be addressed to Paul, Dan, Will, Kev, Andy, Etc.

I was Etc.

Danger Mouse

Around this time, I got my first car. It was a very old Mini with absolutely no suspension, to the point that any woman with boobs bigger than an A size could not sit in the front. If I drove too fast, I used to get a stitch from bouncing up and down. The bonnet also bounced up and down, the latch having fallen off. At first, everyone wanted a lift, but pretty quickly I noticed my friends choosing to get the bus or even walk because being in my car was 'too tiring'.

Ronnie

One day, I was sitting in my flat above the brothel when the phone rang.

'Hello. This is Ronnie Corbett,' said a voice belonging unmistakably to Ronnie Corbett. I let out an excited squeak. I had spent many happy evenings watching *The Two Ronnies* with Nan and Bok. I couldn't believe I was actually talking to Ronnie. His monologues in the chair had always been my favourite part.

Ronnie asked if I would like to write some jokes for him. Although *The Two Ronnies* had finished by now, he performed his monologues live and also on *The Ben Elton Show*.

I was incredibly excited. I have no idea how he got my number and never thought to ask. But we agreed we would meet in a few days and I would give him some jokes. This was before email – and although the crazy futuristic world of faxing had arrived, I couldn't afford one.

We established that we lived about an hour apart (I was in Peckham and he was in Croydon) and we agreed to meet in a lay-by, halfway between us.

So, at the appointed hour, I bounced and clattered up in Danger Mouse and parked in the lay-by. Seconds later, Ronnie, a car enthusiast, glided up in a beautiful Bentley and parked in front of me. We both got out and walked towards each other. I handed him a brown envelope full of jokes, he handed me an envelope full of cash – and we drove off again. It was probably the coolest moment of my life.

Debbie

A few years after I started writing, another woman arrived on the scene. Her name was Debbie. I was thrilled to see a whole other woman. I couldn't wait to work with her. Of course, that never happened. Producers might have wanted/allowed one woman to work in a writers' room – but why on earth would you need two? That would be ridiculous.

Also, due to the reclusive nature of writers, we didn't bump into each other. But I admired her from afar. She was incredibly prolific and very funny. When I was bringing *Spitting Image* to its knees, I asked her to submit sketches – which she did. And I would occasionally see both our names on the credits of other sketch shows and realise we were submitting material to the same show. She usually called herself D. A. Barham – so that people would judge her work objectively and not be prejudiced by the fact she was a woman.

Seeing how the business responded to her was enlightening. It made me realise that people must have been having similar conversations about me. People commented on her looks, her weight, her age, her background, the fact that she had never been to university. People were at best surprised and at worst dismissive of the fact that this young woman had left home in Sheffield and come to London at the age of seventeen and was quickly getting more commissions than her male Oxbridge contemporaries.

But as I watched and admired Debbie from afar and envied her prolific output, I noticed something. She was getting thinner. And thinner. She was disappearing before my very eyes. Many writers enjoy the feeling of being invisible, but Debbie was taking it to extremes.

My sightings of Debbie were sporadic. The BBC would hold ghastly annual drinks parties and I could rarely persuade myself to get dressed and leave the house to attend – so years would pass without me seeing her. But each time I did, her physical appearance had altered dramatically.

'Don't disappear!' I wanted to say. 'That's what they want!'

But I didn't say it.

And the next time I had to force myself to get dressed and leave the house and mingle with other writers was at Debbie's funeral. She was twenty-six.

Mincing around the bush

I'm not good at talking about my feelings. I have a habit of under-sharing. If only there was an easier way than talking. Maybe I should learn semaphore – then I would be able to discuss all my maritime or nautical issues.

One day a friend of mine asked me how I felt about something and got so exasperated at my evasive response that she shouted, 'STOP MINCING AROUND THE BUSH!' In her fury she had combined 'mincing words' with 'beating around the bush'. But actually, 'mincing around the bush' is the perfect description of how I express my feelings.

Fatty

I was excited to write for Jo Brand. She is hilarious, wise and a truly good human being, and it was also my first time writing for a female performer. I had written from the perspective of a lot of men – and I was excited to write jokes about life from a female point of view.

I noticed that within a few seconds of coming on stage, Jo would make a comment about her appearance or her weight. For example: 'I must be an anorexic, because an anorexic looks in the mirror and sees a fat person.' I felt that she had covered the whole weight/appearance thing and maybe I could write some jokes for her about other things. But I was told that if she didn't mention her weight or her appearance in the first few seconds, someone would shout something abusive at her and it was better to pre-empt that because being publicly humiliated is not a good way to start an act.

It wasn't just audience members; critics were as bad. Gary Bushell in *The Sun* described her as a 'hideous old boiler'. In print. In a national newspaper. And so my first experience of writing for a woman was to write jokes about how fat she was.

Open-and-shut case

One morning I was woken up by a constant ringing on my doorbell. Assuming it was a customer with an urgent need for Flat A, I ignored it. But it didn't stop so eventually I stumbled downstairs in my pyjamas to find two workmen who had been sent by the landlord to fix the door.

I let them in and went upstairs to make them a cup of tea. When I returned, they had gone and so had the door.

I stood holding two cups of tea and watching the traffic go by while the situation sank in. This is why no one should have let me be a grown-up. I wasn't prepared for dealing with things like this.

'Blue,' I said, when the policeman asked me to describe the door.

'Anything else?'

'With a letter box in the middle,' I added.

Soon the landlord and the women from Flat A were surrounding me.

'Are you an idiot?' one asked.

'Yes!' I exclaimed. 'Obviously!'

Finally I felt understood.

Lenny

Writing for Lenny Henry was wonderful. His comedy
was dismissed for a long time as 'not funny' by the
white comedians who, at the time, were busy embracing
'laddishness'. And for some weird reason he was blamed
for the racism that surrounded the fact that the only
job he could get on TV as a newcomer was on *The Black
and White Minstrel Show*. But to be in the mostly black
audience at one of his shows, and to feel the palpable
sense of joy, excitement and relief that someone was
finally talking about their lives and their experiences,
was something I'll never forget.

Hashtag

It can be difficult working in a male-dominated industry.
It can also be absolutely fine. And I have never known
anything else. But there are times when you are
overlooked, your work is scrutinised and criticised in a
way your male colleagues' isn't, and your appearance,
clothes and relationship status are also discussed and
evaluated in a way that doesn't happen to your male
colleagues.

Occasionally, I have been treated with outright
hostility. One producer who made it very clear he didn't
want me on the show 'bumped' into me when we were
alone in a corridor and sent me flying. And then there are
the other experiences.

Every single woman I have ever met has at least one
#MeToo experience. Here's one of mine.

I was twenty-five at the time. And I got asked to work
on a show with a sixty-year-old man. He was one of my
comedy heroes and had worked on a lot of shows with a
lot of other comedy heroes of mine, so I was very excited.

The filming was happening outside of London, so the
whole crew were staying in a hotel. As is often the case
with filming, the hours were very long, so we would work
all day and then go back to the hotel just to sleep.

One the first night, I got into the lift to go to my room
and He got in with me. As soon as the doors closed, he
grabbed me, pushed me against the wall and stuck his
tongue down my throat. His hands were everywhere. I
froze in shock and fear. When the lift doors opened, I just

about had the presence of mind to wriggle free from his grip and run to my room and lock the door.

As I stood, leaning against my door, feeling horrible and guilty and ashamed, the phone rang. It was Him telling me he was in his room, naked and waiting. I hung up.

I couldn't eat or sleep. I didn't want to go back to work and face him, but I didn't know what else to do.

The next day I went into work and acted as though nothing had happened. At the end of that day, I got into the lift alone. Just as the doors were closing, he jumped in. The same thing happened again.

I was furious with myself and felt like an idiot.

Again I stayed awake all night, wondering what to do.

The next day, I went to the female producer and, utterly mortified, said I didn't want to talk about it but if I got in the lift and He got in the lift too, could she get in the lift with me? I fled, humiliated and embarrassed as she stared at me in horror.

That night, I said I was going upstairs to bed and He said he was going to do the same. I turned to the producer I had confided in that morning. She very pointedly turned and looked the other way.

And that is the perfect metaphor for what the whole industry did for decades.

Closure

Twenty-five years later, I was at home when the phone rang and it was Him. I hadn't heard his voice since the incidents all that time ago – but immediately I started shaking. To my amazement, he apologised for what he had done. And to my fury, I heard myself saying it was fine and it didn't matter.

That night, I couldn't eat and I couldn't sleep. I was consumed with self-loathing and confusion. But I tried to tell myself that at least he had apologised. Maybe that was some kind of closure.

Not closure

A week later, the phone rang again. Now in his mid-eighties, he was clearly losing his memory. He had no recollection of our previous conversation and he apologised again. He did so the next week and the next week and the next week and the next week. Not so much closure as a constant reopening of an old wound. It was almost funny, except it wasn't.

Express yourself

My body developed a number of ways of dealing with feelings. I have a permanent stomach ache. That's just a given. Then at moments of extreme happiness or sadness, I have a nosebleed. And if I'm tired or unhappy, I pass out. In certain circumstances I can manage all three at once. The trifecta.

A friend of mine got a job in a school for children with disabilities. One of the girls needed a wheelchair with a special machine that would enable her to speak. Her mother and friends raised money tirelessly until, after nine months, they had enough for the wheelchair. There was a special unveiling at the school and they finally gave the girl her wheelchair. As soon as she got in it, she started crashing into people and saying 'cunt'. Initially there was a sense of disappointment and embarrassment – everyone had been hoping it would be a joyful, uplifting moment. But gradually people were happy – the girl was now mobile and able to express herself, and this was clearly what she wanted to say to the world. Which you would, if you'd waited nine months to say it. I admired her honesty. She didn't have the time or the luxury of nosebleeds, she had to get straight to the point.

Shambles

I'd always been a fan of Mel and Sue's live shows and so I was overjoyed when they got their own TV show, *Light Lunch*, and even more excited when they asked me to write on it. The fact that it was live made their shambolic charm even more appealing as every day, somehow, they managed to pull off the impossible. With (I don't think they'd mind me saying) minimal preparation, they would cook meals, interview celebrities and cobble together a totally engaging and funny hour of television, on the hoof. It felt as though we'd stolen the keys to the studio and were having some fun before the grown-ups found out. The adults would try to interfere, sometimes usefully – when informing us it wasn't safe to go in the green room alone (because of 'handsy' guests) – but usually they just wanted to tell us off. They didn't feel we were taking it seriously enough. Because we weren't. And they never really forgave us for our attitude that 'it was only TV'.

Newts

Becoming a homeowner was a proud moment. A rather brief proud moment because it seemed I'd bought a home that was being held together by wallpaper. When I stripped the wallpaper, a wall fell down. Also, when I flushed the loo, the lights went off.

I went and stood in the garden, roof tiles sliding noisily off the roof and raining on my head. In the garden, between two dying trees, I discovered I was the owner of a pond. I'd never wanted a pond, but I soon found out that a pond is a wonderful thing. There were newts in there!

Having grown up in the middle of London, I'm not very well informed when it comes to nature – I was in my thirties before I learnt that sparrows are not baby pigeons – and I had never seen a newt before. They are incredible! They are tiny swimming dinosaurs! It's like travelling back to prehistoric times. They are the most beautiful creatures and I instantly fell in love with them. I spent a lot of time in the garden, avoiding the problems inside my house, and gazing at the carefree newts.

But then I discovered I wasn't the only one who loved the newts. A crow frequently visited our pond. At first, I was delighted. It was like being the owner of an African waterhole, watching all the exotic creatures come by. But then I realised the crow wasn't taking sips of water, he was picking newts out of the pond and pulling their arms and legs off. I was distraught. I tried putting the injured newts back in the pond, but they didn't do so well. They were now more like missiles than newts and just glided straight to the bottom.

I decided to patrol the pond full time. Every time I saw the crow, I would run at it, waving my arms and yelling. The crow wasn't that bothered. It would take one hop backwards, but it wouldn't fly away until I actually tried to rugby-tackle it. The builder who was trying to repair my wall was highly amused.

After a few days of my vigilante patrolling, the crow stopped coming. I was thrilled. My ninja moves had worked. I performed a short but moving ceremony for the bodies and limbs of the newts that had amassed in a rather distressing way by my pond.

Mid-ceremony, the builder came out to find out what was going on.

'No more problems with the crow then?' he asked.

'No. I think I scared him off,' I said, proudly.

'Yeah. It wasn't you,' said the builder. 'I shot him.'

You probably have a lot of questions. I had a lot of questions. Did I ask any of those questions? No. I just said, 'Crikey,' and rushed off.

I don't want to go into details about what I was doing, but when I tell you that soon afterwards all the lights went out, I think you'll know. My anxiety always goes to my stomach.

Later, my neighbour introduced herself over the garden fence and welcomed me to the area.

'Have you met our friendly neighbourhood crow?' she asked.

'No! I haven't seen him! It wasn't me! What crow?' I answered.

It seemed to me the only answer was to move house and start a new life under a new identity. But no one wanted to buy a house held together by wallpaper, where the lights went off if you flushed the loo and where the garden was paved with roof tiles.

Zig-a-zig-ah

Around this time, I was asked to do some work on the film *Spice World* (described by Statler and Waldorf as 'something that not only has absolutely no substance to it but also is difficult to watch'). This was at the very height of their fame. I turned up on set early and already there were hundreds of people outside where we were filming. The filming had hit a snag. The girls had fallen out with each other and were no longer on speaking terms. The producers spotted that I was female and sent me to find out what had happened.

I soon discovered the grave details of the situation.

'Scary always makes us go to the loo with her and then she never waits for us afterwards,' said Ginger Spice. A lament heard through the ages.

Doing my best impression of Henry Kissinger, I sought out Scary Spice and suggested that after going to the loo, she wait for the other Spice Girls. She shrugged. I took this as agreement.

Filming restarted and everyone was jubilant. The producer told me I could go home. But by now, there were thousands upon thousands of fans outside. The police had put barriers up to try to contain them. But the fans were shouting and screaming and trying to push the barriers over.

It was decided it wasn't safe for me, so instead they put me in Scary Spice's black limo with tinted windows and the number plate SCARY. They told the driver to drive me to the nearest Tube station.

The gates opened, the limo emerged and there was a stampede towards the car. Fists thudded on the roof and windows, faces were pressed against the glass. 'I love you!' screamed frenzied fans. I glanced over at the door. Not locked. I prayed nobody would try the handle. If the mob found a puny white girl inside instead of a gorgeous Spice Girl, I was going to get ripped limb from limb. Actually, if I had been a Spice Girl, I think I would have been ripped limb from limb – such was the ferocity of their love. And that, in case you were wondering, is why I did not become a global sensation.

The One

After a series of relationships that were completely wrong for me and made my ovaries want to form a suicide pact, I gave up on finding someone who was right for me and resigned myself to a life alone where I would eventually be found dead, months after actually dying, either melted into my sofa or having my face eaten by cats.

Then of course I accidentally stumbled across The One. It took quite some time to persuade The One that I was also The One, because I turned out to be exactly the opposite of the One she was looking for.

Everyone was very surprised by my choice of partner. Except Ronnie, who said he'd known all along.

When it came to telling The Patriarchy and The Witch about my new partner, I needed to find the right words. I needed to channel Martin Luther King, I needed the vocal dexterity of Socrates, the power of Churchill, the passion of Nelson Mandela. I needed a poetic, majestic and rousing speech. In the end I said: 'I'm seeing someone. It might not be a man.'

Yes, it turned out I had a thyroid problem too.

Drag

The next time I got to write for women was several years later. There was a 'female sketch show' called *Smack the Pony*. This was at a time when 'Are women funny?' was an actual conversation and a lot of people thought a man dressed as a woman was always going to be funnier than a woman. A lot of people still think that, actually.

It was fantastic to be able to write for such brilliant, funny women, but there was such fear from the men at Channel 4 that men might not watch or like the show, that we were encouraged to avoid writing about 'women's subjects' or doing sketches that might put male viewers off. We also had a strict swearing quota. We were allowed a certain number of 'fucks' per series. One week, we blew all our swear words in one sketch so that the following week, when we wanted to say 'motherfucker', we were told we had gone over our allotted swear word rations. We begged to be able to say 'motherfucker'. It went to increasingly important departments for a decision on whether we could say 'motherfucker'. Finally, the answer was given. We couldn't say 'motherfucker' but they would allow us to say 'sisterfucker'. It's interesting that when they looked at the word 'motherfucker', they decided the part that was offensive was 'mother'. What a bunch of sisterfuckers.

Expecting

I'd always wanted to be a parent. For as long as I could remember. I'd had good role models. My own parents, of course – but I also admired the way my Action Man and the Bionic Woman had parented their giant baby. And of course the way Flo had parented Starsky.

I had read all the books – if there were a theory test as well as (or instead of) a pregnancy test, I would have passed with flying colours. It was the practical side of the pregnancy test that let me down. Not the weeing on a stick part. I like to think I am an accomplished wee-er on sticks. I've done it enough. But the result was always negative. I do think the pregnancy test manufacturers are a little blinkered. Why just two options? Why not:

Blue – You are pregnant.
Red – You are not pregnant.
Green – Today is a good day for money matters.

Eventually my doctor referred me for some tests. I was sent to the INFERTILITY CLINIC. That seemed harsh. We didn't know yet. That's like calling the eye clinic the BLIND CLINIC. Or the cancer ward the DEATH CLINIC.

'Give me a chance!' I shouted at the sign. It didn't reply.

The test had to be done on the fourteenth day of my cycle, but the clinic was only open on Tuesdays and you had to book at least three months in advance.

Finally, after two years, the stars aligned and the fourteenth day of my cycle was a Tuesday and I had booked. It was a miracle. I turned up only to find the clinic was closed that day due to staff shortages. I wept. I was asked to move away and weep somewhere else.

Eventually I had all the tests – blood tests, internal ultrasounds, X-rays, dye squirted up my tubes – everything they could think of. And finally, I had an answer. I was unlucky. There was no obvious reason I wasn't getting pregnant; the medical diagnosis was UNLUCKY.

So far, I was doing really badly at parenting. I had failed before I'd even begun. I was such a bad parent, I couldn't even become a parent.

The Circle of Life

There's a certain kind of madness that descends when you are trying to have a baby and failing to have a baby. The dizzying cycle of hope and despair creates an uncomfortable dichotomy. You are empty of baby but pregnant with longing.

I remember watching a news report about a baby being snatched from hospital. I remember the three thoughts I had as I watched the report:

1. Ooh! I should snatch a baby from a hospital!
2. No, I shouldn't do that . . . because I want to actually experience the miracle of childbirth.
3. And also it's wrong.

In *that* order.

My mantra

In difficult times, I often wished I had a guru to consult or a mantra to repeat or a motto to cling to. Nan once said, 'Don't eat jelly before you go to church.' I don't eat jelly and (obviously) I don't go to church, but this always seemed like excellent advice.

Ain't No Party

Writing for S Club 7 was an unexpected turn of events but it got me a LOT of kudos with six-year-olds, which is hard to come by in normal circumstances. It was a bit like being a teacher again. Sometimes I had to take them swimming and, as they kept reminding me, I was old enough to be their mum.

When we were filming their TV show in Spain, we wrote an episode where Jon loved the country so much, he decided to become Spanish and was then called up for National Service. This was because they wanted to do a song-and-dance number in camouflage-coloured outfits.

The BBC executive rejected the script because she said it would give the fans PTSD flashbacks about the Vietnam War. Bearing in mind most of their fans were British children born in the mid-nineties, I felt this was unlikely. But we had to change the script.

Statler and Waldorf described it as 'one of the most fatuous shows on television'. What they didn't mention was that it was the most popular show for people in prison. For reasons it's best not to think about.

Constant craving

Finally, I was pregnant! It turns out making babies is nothing to do with dusty legs. It is a sperm and an egg and a team of scientists and doctors and drugs and implements and temperatures and surges and hormones and then placing some sperm somewhere where your egg can't help but trip over it as it ambles down your fallopian tube. Hey presto! I was knocked up!

I embraced all aspects of pregnancy. I was wearing maternity clothes within the first week. I was awash with hormones. I would find myself crying at adverts – 'he had an accident at work and it wasn't his fault!'

And I had cravings. Lots of cravings. I'd read all about how cravings can mean you are lacking in a certain vitamin or mineral. For example, if you crave oranges, you may need vitamin C. If you crave coal, you may be deficient in minerals. I craved Guinness and a pork pie, which meant I was a working-class man from the North. I also craved a new iPhone, which is a real craving and the baby needs it and it shouldn't be ignored.

I went to antenatal classes. Many, many antenatal classes. At one, my partner, who is known as The Moose, was called 'Dad' and put with the other 'Dads' where they had to build a delivery room out of Lego. Meanwhile, the teacher showed the Mums how to breastfeed our babies by demonstrating with a doll and a knitted nipple. Then she asked if we had any questions. I had so many questions. Who had knitted the nipples? Whose job was Nipple Knitter? How could I apply? What kind of annual nipple turnover was there? How many nipples per day would you need to knit?

I had finally found my calling. I wanted to spend my life being pregnant and knitting nipples.

Thin

Fresh from my triumph on the timeless classic *Spice World*, I thought I should have another go at writing something with no substance that was difficult to watch. With a friend I worked on the film *High Heels and Low Lifes*, which, for those of you who don't remember, was summarised by Statler and Waldorf in the following way: 'The plot was ridiculous, the writing atrocious and the acting bad.'

They went on to describe it as 'thin but entertaining'. Something I would rather like to have on my gravestone.

Names

We bought a book of baby names. But no name seemed good enough for my baby.

Some parents like to name their children after their favourite places – e.g. India, Atlanta. A friend of mine named his children after his favourite islands – e.g. Iona, Skye. I briefly considered Sheppey. Or Dogs. Or where the baby was conceived – Infertility Clinic.

Other parents combine their names to form a new name. Bronwen and Ian becomes . . . Brian. That's not a good example. Mike and Kelly becomes Mike. No, wait. Dave and Veronica becomes Dave. This is actually harder than it looks. Pete and Teresa becomes Pete. OK. Forget that.

Weather front

My favourite things were the scans. Staring at the screen and seeing what looked like a cold weather front coming in from the west.

Sometimes, if I stared really hard, I could see a tiny blurry tadpole standing on its head. That was my baby. It's incredible to me that something so minuscule can cause such enormous changes in your body. It's a tiny tyrant. It's also surprising that when that tiny tyrant dies, your body doesn't always notice. It's too busy being pregnant.

'The heart has stopped beating,' said the doctor.

I looked pregnant, I felt pregnant, I was in some respects pregnant. And yet . . .

I wasn't a mother. I was the opposite of a mother. My womb was a coffin.

POC

I went to hospital. There was no room on the usual ward, so they put me on the maternity ward.

The form I signed said I was having a procedure to remove POC.

'What's a POC?' I asked.

'Product of conception,' was the answer.

That seemed like the worst name of all for my baby.

Split personality

I've often wrestled with the question – who am I? I came round from the 'procedure' and while high on whatever excellent drugs they give you, I talked at length to the nurse about the racism I had suffered growing up black in the Southern States of America. I told her she had it easy. Later I had to go and find her and apologise. She was black and being told she had it easy by a white woman must have been more than a little galling. So now I knew who I was. An absolute twat.

Battle of the sexes

I wanted to get away and go and be alone on a desert island, so we spent all the money we didn't have on a holiday to Barbados.

The first few days, I just stood in the sea, which was warm and womblike. After a few days, we decided to be a bit more adventurous. We asked the receptionist if it was possible to go kayaking. She was surprisingly thrilled by this request. She asked if we had kayaked before. We said yes, a bit, once. She was even more excited and said we could do it on Sunday at exactly 2 p.m. Come to this spot.

It seemed very specific, but we signed a form and agreed to do so.

On Sunday, we were in the middle of lunch when the receptionist came and found us. You're supposed to be kayaking! We had completely forgotten so we ambled over to reception, still chewing. Suddenly we were led to a van and told that Elvis would drive us to the kayaking place. Elvis drove for over an hour. We tried to convey that it wasn't that important – he didn't need to go to all that trouble to take us kayaking – but he said it was an honour.

When we finally reached the destination, we made a hideous discovery. It was the West Indies inter-island kayaking championships and apparently we were representing Barbados. Their team had been two short, and now we had made up the numbers. We were the only women there. Also, had we actually been kayaking before? Or was it canoeing? What's the difference?

I turned to The Moose and said, 'Let's just back slowly into that hedge behind us and hide.'

She nodded. We silently shuffled backwards in the sand. I merged with bush and just as The Moose was about to do the same, a man approached her and said, 'You two should split up because you're weaker than everyone else. I'll take you in my kayak, and she can go with someone else.'

Uh oh.

'No!' I heard The Moose say. 'We're fine. We'll do it together.' Then she hauled me out of the bush and said, 'Now we have to beat that man.'

I hate Making Points and I prefer to admire the Moral High Ground from a distance, but The Moose would not be deterred.

We were all piled onto a boat that then bumped and bounced out to sea for hours. It was extremely choppy. I felt rather peaky. I wished I hadn't eaten such a big lunch. And the rum punch had probably been a mistake.

When we got to the absolute middle of nowhere, the kayaks were thrown into the sea and we were told to jump in and get into them. I wanted to explain that I don't like jumping into water. I like to inch in very slowly. Also, I don't like being out of my depth. Also, I don't – SPLASH! Someone had pushed me into the water. It was FREEZING. I then spent several minutes in a passionate slippery embrace with the kayak as we rolled round and round in the waves. Finally, The Moose tamed the kayak and clambered in and I followed suit.

The starting gun was fired and we started paddling.

163

'Ooh, it's tricky when it's wavy . . .' I started to say.

'PADDLE!' shouted The Moose.

'I keep getting splashed in the face . . .' I added.

'PADDLE!' came the reply.

'It's actually jolly tiring . . .' I observed.

'PADDLE!'

We paddled and paddled and paddled until I thought I was going to die.

'My arms are on fire . . .'

'PADDLE!'

'I think I'm going to faint . . .'

'PADDLE!'

'Is my nose bleeding or is that sea water . . . ?'

'PADDLE!'

We kept paddling. I was missing every other stroke because the waves were knocking us about. We were being fuelled by The Moose's will power.

'Could I just slide into the sea and die, please?'

'PADDLE!'

'You'd be lighter, so you might do better . . .'

'PADDLE!'

'Tell my parents I love them . . .'

'PADDLE!'

By this time, I was slipping in and out of consciousness.

We passed the man who told us we were weak. We passed many, many boats. We came third.

The Moose was exhilarated. We were greeted like heroes. People wanted to high-five us, but I couldn't lift my arm. We were given a commemorative cup, which dropped with a thunk to the floor because I was too weak to hold it. For the rest of the holiday, my arms hung like pieces of string from my shoulders. The Moose was jubilant because she said we had Made a Point. I think the point we had made was that exercise is a very bad idea.

The Michaels

I decided at a young age that I was going to marry
George Michael. We were going to be George and Georgia
Michael. For so many reasons, it was a love that could
never be – but it took me a long time to give up on it.

By this time, some friends and I had started a small
animation company and we were cooped up in a tiny
office in the middle of Soho.

One day I answered the phone and the voice said it was
George Michael. We were working with impressionists
and my obsession with him was well known, so I
presumed it was a joke. But the voice insisted it wasn't
and gave an address to come to.

The next day, my friend Giles and I headed to the
address and found ourselves at a decidedly dodgy-looking
door. We knocked on the door and waited. Eventually it
opened and we were led downstairs to a huge, sumptuous
recording studio. And there he was – my tiny, stubbly
husband-to-be, smoking an enormous joint.

George explained that he wanted us to animate a video for his new track. He asked if we wanted to hear the track. We nodded dumbly.

He turned on some music so loudly that my ear drums had a seizure. He then watched us as we listened. Not sure how to react, we started nodding our heads, clicking our fingers and tapping our feet, trying to look cool. It was excruciating.

George had a lot of things he wanted to say about politics, about Tony Blair, about George Bush and about the Iraq war. I wished he would just wiggle his tiny leather-clad hips but he didn't want to be in the video. So we animated his thoughts about Tony Blair, about George Bush and about the Iraq war and contributed to one of his worst-selling singles of all time. Nobody wanted to hear what he thought about politics, they just wanted him to wiggle his tiny leather-clad hips. People are shallow, ignorant idiots. And when I say people, I very much mean me.

Handbag

I eventually got pregnant again. This time I was too scared to wear maternity clothes or look at name books or go to antenatal classes.

I went to scans and closed my eyes. My bedside cabinet was pregnant with baby books that I dared not get out.

A friend suggested it was a good idea when pregnant to go and get a bra fitted. I did this and it was a good idea only in that it got me used to the idea of strangers looking at and handling my breasts, as that happens a lot once you have a baby. She also warned me that my nipples might change colour. Correct. They turned brown. The good news was, they now matched my handbag. The bad news was, in a few months they would be bigger than my handbag.

Making history

When it became legal to have a civil partnership, we had one. I was eight months pregnant at the time. I like to think ours was the first shotgun civil partnership in history.

As the registrar declared we were now civilly partnered, The Moose leaned towards me and whispered, 'You've hit the jackpot with me, you know. I'm way out of your league.'

X-rated

Every single broadcaster in this country has told me that they 'already have a show with women in it' when I have suggested shows with women in the lead.

One day I went for a meeting with two producers and one of them played a sex tape of Pamela Anderson and Tommy Lee that he had managed to get hold of. It was strange watching porn with these two men I barely knew. All I can remember is getting the distinct impression that Pammy wasn't enjoying herself. And neither was I. They never asked me what my idea was.

Hiccups

Whoever says you are pregnant for nine months is lying. It is forty weeks. Plus another couple of weeks if you're late. That's almost for ever. I felt every single second of every single minute of every single hour of every single day of those weeks.

The last few months were hell. I was massive. My bladder was the size of a walnut. Sneezing was not an option. I couldn't see my feet – or indeed anything else below waist level. I would find myself asking The Moose, 'Am I wearing any knickers?' It's important to decide whether your partner is a trustworthy person before you answer the door to Amazon.

I spent a considerable percentage of my life going to the loo. If I had a penny for every time I spent a penny – I'd have 0p – but that's not the point, the point is . . . it's relentless.

The baby wouldn't let me walk too fast. He would anxiously put his foot on some kind of internal brake to make me slow down. He wouldn't let me sleep on my right side. He would just elbow me in the ribs until I moved. He would get hiccups at 2 a.m. and they would last for hours. I loved every second of it. It meant he was still there. In fact, I'd focused so much of my mind and energy on keeping him there that then he wouldn't come out.

Labour

There are many theories on the best way to bring on labour. For example: a curry, a cocktail and a shag. It would be nice if that worked because that may well have been how you got pregnant in the first place. In fact, the gel that is used in hospitals to induce labour does contain sperm. However, if the doctor suggests he apply this gel with his penis, seek a second opinion.

Birth is a beautiful thing. If your idea of beauty is a tractor pulling a combine harvester out of your vagina. Having your labour induced is like putting a turbo thruster on the tractor.

A friend of mine had assembled the most beautiful cherrywood box that opened out into three shelves of perfect little bottles of homeopathic remedies to help with each stage of labour. I was sceptical about how useful this would be, but I was wrong. She used the beautiful cherrywood box to try to club her partner to death during labour. Finally, she was given enough pethidine to make her relax her grip on the beautiful cherrywood box and it was wrestled away from her.

Polite

They say that when you give birth, your primal instinct kicks in. Friends had told me stories of bellowing like a beast, howling at the top of their lungs, shouting abuse at anyone who crossed their field of vision.

I had a similar experience. My primal instinct is Not to Make a Fuss and to Be Polite at All Costs.

As the contractions intensified to unendurable agony, the doctor and The Moose were deep in conversation about types of lichen found in the Shetland Islands.

I raised my hand.

'Sorry to interrupt, but the baby is coming out of my body,' I said politely, as the baby's head appeared.

Then I lost consciousness.

Motherhood

Motherhood is not like it is in the adverts. I thought it would involve a lot of being wrapped in white cashmere, lying on a white bed in a white room asleep with my perfect baby asleep in front of me.

In fact, the first day I got home, I was too weak to walk, so I fell asleep lying on the hall floor, wearing paper pants, with my head on the bottom stair.

Headbutt

Nobody tells you that motherhood involves a lot of being headbutted by your baby. And cutting them out of their babygrows when they do explosive poos. And that you will also have delivered piles almost as big as your baby – and yet when you put a bonnet on one, nobody congratulates you.

My baby was ENORMOUS. He had rugby player's thighs and arms like Popeye. The Patriarchy said he was terrifying and The Witch peered into his cot and let out a scream. They started referring to him as The Speck.

Breastfeeding is an incredible thing. And also a painful, frustrating and dispiriting thing. Breast pumps are used a lot these days and they are designed to make you lose the will to live.

Looking at your post-birth body will be a bit like revisiting the neighbourhood you grew up in. It will seem terribly familiar and yet very different at the same time. Everything will be bigger – or smaller – and there will be a Starbucks on the corner. A metaphorical one, you understand. If there's a real one, seek medical help.

Chromosomes

As I persisted in having the wrong chromosomes, I was finding it very difficult to get any shows commissioned. So instead I managed to get jobs on other people's shows so that I could ruin those for them instead. I wrote episodes of *My Family* (hailed as 'an unholy abomination' and 'puerile, unimaginative DROSS') and *Not Going Out* ('limp, undercooked, engineered farce'), among others. The producers were not always thrilled to have me on the team, but I enjoyed the challenge of trying to win them round. I remember the pride I felt when one said, 'This isn't actually the worst thing I've ever read.'

Gardening with body parts

After burping The Speck one day and putting him down to sleep, I became aware of a terrible smell. This was not unusual but for once it wasn't his nappy. He hadn't been sick. It wasn't the nappy mountain in the bedroom. I was perplexed.

The smell seemed to be following me around. As I opened the door to Amazon, confidently be-knickered, I caught sight of myself in the mirror. And there, on my shoulder, was the rotting umbilical cord stump that had fallen off my baby.

'Oh, sorry,' I said, trying to casually brush the festering flesh off myself. 'Belly button,' I explained to the delivery man. I never saw him again.

Later, I was at my friend's house. She was the perfect mother. She jogged while she was pregnant. I barely moved. She gave birth naturally in her home. I had drugs, forceps, cuts, stitches – everything going. She was producing too much milk for her baby. I was struggling to rustle up elevenses. She seemed to know exactly what she was doing and I was always asking for her advice. But for once, she asked me for advice. She had just had her son circumcised and asked me where in her garden she should bury the foreskin. I looked out of the window. 'Maybe over by that tree?' I suggested.

'No, I can't put it there. That's where his placenta is.'

That's when I realised that not only did I know nothing about gardening with body parts, but I was totally inadequate – as a mother and as a human being.

Not up to the job

I became convinced that I wasn't a good mother. I had wanted to be one for so long and yet now I couldn't seem to get the hang of it at all. The Speck seemed unimpressed by my attempts at parenting.

He was not interested in my games of peek-a-boo. He didn't listen when I read him a book. He stared past me, looking for something more interesting when I spoke to him. And most tellingly of all, he wouldn't call me Mummy. I imagined it was because I hadn't earned it yet.

I longed for him to call me Mummy. I longed for it, dreamed about it and, quite shamelessly, tried to make it happen.

'Mummy,' I would say, pointing at myself.

'Mum,' I would offer, as an alternative.

'Mumma,' I would suggest.

The Speck would stare blankly back.

'OK. Forget it,' I said, one day, thoroughly defeated. 'It's time to get off the bus. We're in Peckham.'

'Peckham,' said The Speck, quite clearly.

I was thrilled and enraged. His first word! He'd said his first word!! His first word was . . . Peckham.

'Peckham?' I said. 'You won't say Mummy but you'll say Peckham?'

The Speck stared blankly back.

'Say it again,' I said, suddenly desperate for him to repeat it.

178

'Peckham! Peckham! Peckham!' I repeated.

'Why are you trying to get your child to say Peckham?' asked an interested passenger.

Because I wanted to hear his voice again.

Supreme Leader

I finally had my own show commissioned (by a woman)! It was exciting and petrifying and ultimately described by Statler and Waldorf as 'awful in every way' and 'the latest in a series of sitcoms that plumb such depths that they would need a Robert Ballard expedition to find where they end'.

There is something thrilling but utterly terrifying about seeing hundreds of people working to bring something to life. Something that started with you putting pen to paper. People have questions and I am expected to have answers – lots of them. It's the old 'exuding' problem again.

Around this time I started having a new anxiety dream in which Kim Jong-Un has died. Strictly speaking, that isn't the bit that worries me. It's what happens next that is the problem. By some quirk of North Korean inheritance laws, I am made Supreme Leader of North Korea. This doesn't turn out well for anyone. I don't mind what people wear or how their hair is cut or what they do with their spare time and I don't want people marching past and saluting me.

'Just try and enjoy it,' says the Vice Chairman of the Supreme People's Assembly to me.

'I'm trying!' I say to him.

I think I hear a tut.

Kissing trains

The Speck was the most beautiful baby in the world. That goes without saying. When we entered a room, I was convinced that an awe-inspired hush swept across the people gathered. And was that a multitude of angels singing in the background as their eyes alighted on my child?

Well, no, probably not, because looking back at photos I see a very fat, bald baby with bad skin, cradle cap and a worried expression on his face.

I loved him so much I thought I might pop. I missed him when he was asleep and waited impatiently for him to wake. I kissed him so often I worried he might start to erode.

In return, The Speck was inscrutable. But I did notice that he got very anxious when I went out of the room. And when I left the house, he made me kiss each one of his trains hello when I got back.

He had a lot of trains.

Second word

After Peckham, I was keen to get The Speck to say his second word. Mummy, perhaps? Just a suggestion, off the top of my head.

No. No chance. I tried everything.

The breakthrough came when I gave him my phone to play with. He somehow managed to text someone I didn't know very well the word 'buuuuuuurp', which seemed appropriate. Later, he paid the congestion charge. Presumably he had popped into town in his walker.

It seemed typical of that generation to text before they can speak.

Quack quack

By the age of eighteen months, The Speck had a four-word vocabulary (Peckham, bic, me, baa). Then, overnight, it increased by 25 per cent. Actually it increased by 50 per cent because his new word was 'quack quack'. This is a very useful word to have in your vocabulary. You'd be surprised how often it comes up.

Mumbling

The other people who have limited vocabulary are those in positions of power in the TV industry. I was becoming used to being ignored, interrupted, shouted over or insulted. I kind of enjoyed the challenge, having to prove myself, work harder, bounce back, develop a thicker skin.

But there was another kind of sexism too. One that is harder to identify and I think more pernicious. Shows and departments and companies and channels are often run by awkward, mumbling, socially inept men who don't like making eye contact. I noticed this because I like to think of myself as an awkward, mumbling and socially inept person and yet I wasn't allowed into the inner sanctum. And it wasn't because they don't like women or they think women can't write or aren't as good as men, it's because they want to work with other awkward, mumbling, socially inept men because they feel more comfortable with them. Women make them uncomfortable. And that isn't a hate crime. But it is a problem.

Sing!

I discovered that if I pointed at a picture of a sheep,
The Speck wouldn't say 'sheep'. But if I sang 'Baa, baa,
black . . .' he would finish the line of the song and say
'sheep'.

I was so excited. I sang it again and again. I tried to
focus everything on that moment. To hear what his voice
sounded like in that one syllable – it might be a clue to
who he was, to his personality, to how I could reach him.

Soon, he wouldn't go to sleep unless I sang, he wouldn't
eat unless I sang, he wouldn't let me dress him or change
his nappy unless I sang. I sang all day and most of the
night. My voice was hoarse with singing. I sounded like
Tina Turner after a two-hundred-date tour.

Hat

I bought The Speck a new hat for summer. I didn't think he'd agree to wear it, but not only did he wear it, he refused to take it off. He wore it all day and then in the bath. I tried offering him biscuits in exchange for the hat but he refused. At bedtime, he held on to it with both hands so I decided to wait until he was asleep.

Every hour between 7 p.m. and 2 a.m. I tiptoed into his bedroom only to find he was still gripping on to his hat. Finally, at 3 a.m. he had let go and the hat was mine. I felt triumphant. And then tired. And then ridiculous. And then a bit like I should give the hat back. Which I did, at breakfast. He was very pleased.

New shoes

While the other children in our Mothers and Babies group were walking and crawling, The Speck stayed resolutely immobile.

I wondered if having some shoes might help him. He could manage a few steps with me holding his hand, but it was winter and there were puddles and he was in his socks.

I took him to the shoe shop. The assistant asked how old he was.

'Nineteen months,' I replied.

'So he's walking,' she said.

'Yes,' I lied. I don't know why.

'Let's see,' she said.

I panicked.

'What? Now? Right now? Because we're quite busy. Couldn't you just bring us the shoes and we'll pay and go?'

But she insisted.

I put The Speck on the floor. He sat down and didn't move.

I willed him to walk. I prayed for a miracle.

We looked at The Speck. He looked at us. I suggested he wasn't in the mood. But the woman looked sceptical.

She declared in a rather snooty voice that as he wasn't walking, he could only have pre-walking shoes.

I left, chastened. The Speck didn't care. As I pushed him in his buggy, he admired his feet all the way home.

Breakthrough

Somehow, I had managed to get pregnant again. (I got drunk, I went to the fertility clinic, one thing led to another . . .) I was thrilled and excited and scared and delighted.

Out came the maternity clothes, out came the books, out came the strange pillow shaped like an enormous slice of cheese. I couldn't believe it was happening again!

I went for the twelve-week scan.

'The heart has stopped beating,' said the doctor.

I couldn't believe it was happening again.

I went to the hospital. People expected me to be OK with it. After all, I was used to it. It's what I did. But I wasn't OK with it. I felt worse. This time I knew what I was losing.

I came out of hospital. I felt awful. But that seemed to be expected. We decided to drive The Speck to visit his grandmother. But on the journey, I realised I felt awful in a different way. I had a raging temperature, my body ached, I was shaking and I felt sick.

We turned round and started heading back to the hospital as fast as we could. I grabbed a plastic bag that was full of nappies and baby food for The Speck and dumped out the contents. Then I threw up in the plastic bag.

This turned out to be the funniest thing The Speck had ever seen. He laughed loudly, he looked right at me, he engaged, we connected, it was incredible. As we drove, I continued to throw up and The Speck continued to roar with laughter.

It was simultaneously the best and worst moment of my life.

Steak and kidney

There is no problem, according to The Patriarchy, that can't be solved with a hearty meal. In times of crisis, he is on hand to rustle up a little something at any time of the day or night.

A few days later, The Patriarchy and The Witch came to visit. I was still throwing up.

'Oh please don't mention food,' I thought as I saw his sticky-up hair and her hat coming up the stairs.

'I've brought you a little stew with some very spicy chorizo in it . . .' began The Patriarchy.

I immediately had to go to the bathroom, where things shot out of my body with alarming speed.

Once I was an empty shell, I emerged again.

'Are you all right?' asked The Patriarchy. 'Is there anything I can get you?'

'No, thank you,' I said quickly.

'Steak and kidney?' he asked, hopefully, thinking that's what I'd said.

And back into the bathroom I went.

Bins

The Speck suddenly got the hang of walking! I think it was a mistake. He was hanging on to the sofa and he lost his balance, so he suddenly went veering off and did a whole circuit of the room at a very precarious angle. I rushed him out and together we strolled casually past the snooty woman in the shoe shop. Then I decided to take him to the zoo to put some faces to those animal noises. It didn't go well. The thing he was most excited about was the bins. He rushed up and hugged each bin as though it was a long-lost friend. When I tried to steer him towards some majestic animals, he clung on to the bin, crying.

Finally I prised him away from the bin and took him to the butterfly tent. This was a success. He was enchanted by the plastic doors. He ran through the tent, swatting beautiful butterflies out of the way to get to the plastic doors. Once he had caused several different species of endangered butterfly to actually become extinct, I decided it was time to move on.

We went to the gorilla enclosure next. All the gorillas were out and were eating and playing and making tools. It was fascinating. Sadly, The Speck saw none of this as he was pressed against the glass of the enclosure opposite. Which was empty. Except for a woman sweeping. The Speck thought the woman sweeping was the most amazing thing he had ever seen. He watched her for about fifteen minutes until she became so self-conscious, she went and hid. By now it was time to go home, so we left, stopping only to say goodbye to every single bin in the zoo.

Rare

We took The Speck to a rare breeds farm – more opportunities for animal noises. He was sitting in his buggy admiring an emu when the emu bent down and grabbed his whole arm in its beak. I quickly pushed him and the buggy out of beak's reach. As I turned round, I saw The Moose try to punch the emu. It was a good right hook. But the emu just bent its bendy neck and avoided her flailing fist.

Later, The Speck was feeding some chickens and one of the chickens pecked him. I quickly lifted him out of harm's way – only to turn and see my partner giving the chicken a swift kick up the backside. Not really the kind of thing you're meant to do in a farm for protected animals. As The Speck went around the country loving and stroking animals, his parents followed, punching and kicking them.

Sausage

When The Speck was two, I took him to nursery. He was wearing his shiny coat and his new shiny shoes. He insisted on carrying a little briefcase. We arrived to find that his class were doing music and movement and were all rolling round the floor in their pants and vests. The Speck refused to join in and stood in the doorway looking like a door-to-door salesman. After a while he sat in the corner and did paperwork till they'd finished.

When I picked The Speck up, I stood in line with a group of anxious parents. As each child was delivered to their parent, the teacher announced the biggest triumph of the day to murmurs of approval from the other parents and occasionally a short burst of applause.

One day I stood in line hearing:

'She recited the alphabet.'

'He drew a picture of a dinosaur.'

'She wrote a poem about you.'

When it got to my turn the teacher said:

'He licked a sausage.'

I punched the air and shouted, 'YESSSSS!'

There were no murmurs of approval, no bursts of applause. They didn't seem to realise what an achievement this was.

Glamour

Being on set is a strange experience. I always feel like I'm the only one who hasn't got anything to actually *do*. Everyone is so busy and so focused. I often think how much fun it must be to be one of the make-up artists – they know everyone and everything. The prop makers are like magicians, summoning props out of thin air when needed. The costume designers have their huge warm trucks full of rails and rails of clothing. The boom operators are always right in the thick of it. The caterers get to be surrounded by delicious food all day. But I can't apply make-up, I can't make things, I don't know about clothes, my arms are too weedy and I can't cook.

'What do you do?' I ask a man next to me by the monitor, as we filmed a scene set in a garden.

'I'm the worm wrangler,' he says proudly. 'What about you?'

'I'm the . . . word wrangler,' I say, trying to make it sound more exciting.

He looks at me with a mixture of kindness and pity and turns back to the monitor where one of his worms is, in my opinion, hamming it up a little.

Llamas

Pet shop was The Speck's favourite thing to eat. He put it on his chips. The Fat Controller was what we used to change channels on the TV. And 'Crocodile Baby' was one of his favourite songs ('Rockabye Baby').

Fire llama was one of the noises he didn't like. Also car llamas and smoke llamas.

I was pleased he had learnt some new words. I just wished they were the right ones. Although I also wished we lived in a world where llamas would inform us of impending danger.

The test

The doctor suggested the reason The Speck wasn't speaking was that he had a hearing problem. That made sense and I was furious with myself that I hadn't thought of it. That explained why he seemed to be ignoring me and why he heard 'pet shop' instead of 'ketchup' and 'fire llama' instead of 'fire alarm'.

So the following week, I took The Speck for a hearing test. It was a very strange experience. There was a bad-tempered nurse and a depressed man. The depressed man sat opposite us and was meant to entertain/distract The Speck silently. In fact what he did was put a clown's nose on his face, sigh deeply and stare at the table. He looked utterly despondent. Meanwhile the bad-tempered nurse made clicky and whirry noises in The Speck's ear with an instrument. The first couple of times she did this, The Speck looked round, but he quickly realised that when he heard the clicky whirry noise, there was nothing to see but a bad-tempered nurse scowling at him. So after that he ignored her. This completely flummoxed the nurse, so next she whispered, 'Do you want a biscuit?' in his ear. The Speck turned and smiled and said, 'Please.' But she had no biscuit. The Speck, understandably, was outraged. The next time she made a clicky whirry noise, he rather pointedly put his fingers in his ears. This enraged the nurse, who said he was 'not normal' and she couldn't do the hearing test. So we left, leaving the nurse grumbling to herself and the depressed man to his existential crisis. Still with clown nose on.

We hadn't learnt much about his hearing, but we had established that he's very discerning.

Gravel

After my ovaries had been put under close surveillance
by a large group of specialists for several months, I
managed to get pregnant again. It was a team effort. This
was the fourth (and, we decided, last) time.

I felt guilty about The Speck. He didn't know what
was coming. We decided to take him away for a weekend
before the baby arrived.

We went to a hotel for families. There was a swimming
pool and a lovely big warm wooden barn with every toy
you could ever want. We didn't go in the swimming pool
because The Speck didn't like getting wet. And we didn't
go in the big warm barn because The Speck didn't like
other children. Instead we stood outside in the biting
wind while he played with gravel. He had a lovely time.
I was just looking for an animal carcass to crawl into for
warmth.

Not a guinea pig

I had another (gigantic) baby (called The Scrap by my parents). I couldn't believe my luck. He was enormous. I must have a womb like a Tardis.

The Speck came to see the baby. He wasn't sure. I think he was hoping for a guinea pig and this was not a guinea pig. He really liked the fan in my room. There were lots of buttons to press and he thought it was much more fun than a baby. The baby was going to have to convince The Speck that he was better value than a fan or a guinea pig.

Annoying

When The Scrap was just a couple of months old, The Speck developed a habit of getting up at 4 a.m. I wasn't a fan of this habit, especially as The Scrap was waking several times a night for feeds.

The Moose, at this point, would sleep through the feeds and then stagger downstairs at 11 a.m. when I had been up for SEVEN HOURS and tell me how tired she was. I sent her to the doctor and told her to tell him she was being REALLY FUCKING ANNOYING.

She came back with the news that he had examined her and felt 'a mass'. Mass is not a word you ever want to hear, unless you're a nun.

The next few weeks were a blur of scans and blood tests and endless, endless waiting rooms. Finally, we were told she had six malignant tumours and it had spread to her liver and was incurable.

I remember thinking that I hoped she died in an amusing way so that I could turn it into a funny anecdote and therefore be able to tell people she was dead, because I wasn't very good at talking about difficult things.

We went home and sat on the floor with the boys. It was almost unbearable for The Moose to look at them or be with them. She tried to tell me where the gas bills were kept and where the stopcock was and how to read the meter – but I couldn't take in any of it.

More tests followed as they tried to work out how and whether to treat her. I seemed to spend every day running down hospital corridors, finding lost medical records, googling symptoms, arguing with doctors and pushing the boys round in a double-decker buggy.

Several weeks later, it emerged it hadn't spread to her liver, and maybe there was hope. They decided to operate.

The operation took twelve hours. I was told she might not survive it. I pushed the double buggy round and round the block.

When she finally came out of surgery, I didn't recognise her. She looked like she had been dropped from the top of a very tall building.

'Are you sure it's her?' I asked the nurse. She wasn't sure if I wasn't sure. We waited for her to come round to find out.

It was her.

A miracle

Visiting The Moose in hospital over the next few weeks, I became very aware of the other people in the ward. There was a woman opposite The Moose who never had any visitors and never seemed to wake up. I worried about her. Who was she? What had happened? Should I go and talk to her?

One time, The Moose was asleep so I decided I would go and sit with the woman opposite. But just then, three people walked purposefully onto the ward and stood around her bed. They started praying for her. The prayers got louder and louder until they were shouting, 'IN THE NAME OF JESUS, GET UP! STAND UP AND WALK!'

I was praying just as fervently that she wouldn't get up and walk, because I was pretty sure that would go badly.

'LORD, HEAL THIS WOMAN!' they continued. 'IN THE NAME OF JESUS, I *COMMAND* YOU TO STAND UP AND WALK!'

I watched with interest. Was the voice of God going to bellow 'Get the fuck out of bed!' as it had once before? But it didn't. And gradually, the prayers became quieter, less forceful, less confident. And the three people left.

A couple of weeks later I went to bring The Moose home from hospital. The doctors had made a startling discovery. The tumours which had looked malignant and 'acted' malignant were not malignant. It was unbelievable. It was a miracle. She had some incredibly rare condition that only a few people in the world had.

That was more believable. In fact, that was entirely bloody typical.

'So she's not going to die?' I asked.

'No,' they said.

'But you promised me!' I said, shaking my fist.

At this rate I'm never going to get my hands on her Interesting Pebble collection.

Weirdo

Don't tell her I said this, but The Moose is a fucking
weirdo. She likes people. She talks to them. She's
hospitable. I mean, she literally invites people over, to
the house, for extended periods of time. I know! What
is the matter with her? To make matters worse, she
talks to them about her feelings. What the actual fuck?
Sometimes, I'm in the bathroom, holding a flannel to
my nose, and I can hear her talking about her emotions.
What a freak.

I've explained to her, countless times, that feelings are
like pickled eggs – best left unopened, no matter how
drunk you are.

Then what you do (and you may need a pen and paper
for this) is you put the 'pickled eggs' in a box. And then
you put them in a larger box. And then you put them in
a lead-lined box. And then you bury it in some concrete
beneath a volcano (can be metaphorical) and then you
will be absolutely *fine*.

Heartburn

While The Moose was wanging on about her feelings, I was back to normal the very next day. I was totally fine. Although I did feel a little bit sick. But just in my neck.

Then it got worse – it felt like I was being choked. It felt like someone had their hand around my throat. I took a pill for heartburn. It didn't help.

Black cloud

Also I was having trouble with my eyes. It was summer but everything seemed darker. There was literally a black cloud around everything I looked at. But a black cloud that meant I needed to wear sunglasses because everything was murky but also glary. I had my eyes tested.

> They were fine
> I could even read
> the bottom
> line

Bad dreams

I started to have bad dreams. And when I say bad, I mean rubbish. Straight-to-video dreams. I would dream that I was going to see a therapist, but I couldn't get through the door because I was carrying a lot of large baggage. It was like symbolism for dummies. My lazy, lazy subconscious couldn't come up with anything better than that. Freud would have despised me. I was ashamed of my slumbering self.

I would also dream that I was carrying a plate and that people kept putting too many things on it. What on earth could it mean? We'll never know.

Operation

Meanwhile the doctor said that The Speck needed grommets to help with his hearing. The thought of such a small child having to have an operation was horrifying to me, but the doctor said that The Speck couldn't hear and once he had the operation, words would come pouring out of him. He said he'd known children start speaking full sentences within weeks. So we agreed to have it done and found ourselves back in hospital again.

On the day of the operation, we put The Speck in his tiny hospital gown and waited to be called to theatre. We carried him down to the operating room and the nurse explained that, to administer the anaesthetic, I would have to sit The Speck on my knee and hold a mask over his face to send him to sleep.

I tried, but The Speck did not want to have a mask over his face, so we ended up struggling for minutes in what felt like a fight to the death until his body became limp.

Then he was wheeled into the operating theatre.

When he came out an hour later, he was crying inconsolably. It was astonishing to hear him using his voice so loudly – on the rare occasions he spoke, it was always very softly. He looked at me with such outrage and fury, I wished I could explain to him that it had to be done. It was going to change everything.

Muffle

Meanwhile I was having trouble with my hearing too.
The world was muted. Voices were too loud but I couldn't
make out what they were saying. It was like listening
to an out-of-tune foreign radio station. All static and
monotonous urgency.

I went for my own hearing test.

'Your hearing is perfect,' said the doctor in a muffled,
barely audible voice.

Ticket office

Only a few days after the operation, The Speck learnt a new phrase – 'ticket office'. I was very impressed. He said it all day. And then for the next five days he said nothing but 'ticket office'.

Giraffe

The Speck has always been an expert on animals and animal noises. His favourite thing was some slippers he was given with a furry dog on them.

But now, every morning when I put them on his feet, he'd say 'giraffe'. He said it so convincingly that I didn't dare disagree. He used to know the word 'dog'.

Bums

The Speck had clearly got in with the wrong crowd at nursery. He came home knowing the word 'bum'. As if that wasn't bad enough, he quickly realised that saying 'two bums' was twice as rude. Gradually, as the day wore on, the bums increased, until by bedtime we were at 'ten bums'. But that wasn't enough – he wanted to be ruder! The best he could offer was 'ten bums and another bum'.

He used to know the word 'eleven'.

Words

The words hadn't come pouring out of The Speck since the operation. If anything, he seemed to be losing words by the day. We were referred to another doctor. We went, anxious that The Speck might have to have further operations or that he might need a hearing aid.

'It's quite obvious he has autism,' said the doctor, almost before we had sat down. 'He probably won't ever speak. Or do anything. You should put him in an institution.'

I lost all my words. I couldn't speak. I couldn't comprehend. I couldn't process what she was saying.

'And don't have any more children,' she added.

'But I already do,' I said.

Chicken

I once read that a tornado can pick a chicken up, and that the pressure inside the tornado will pluck out its feathers. Then the tornado will dump it, naked, goosebumpy and traumatised, miles from home. This is how I felt. Raw and naked and confused – recently spat out by a terrible tempest in my brain.

Inhale

I went to the doctor. I told her breathing seemed a bit tricky. I didn't tell her that I'd forgotten how to breathe. That I was being sat on by a huge, gloomy black bear. That my lungs were squashed. That I couldn't breathe in. And when I did, the breath came in gasps. That I couldn't breathe out. And when I did, the breath came out as a soundless scream.

She listened to my chest. Everything 'seemed in order'. She gave me an inhaler.

Occasionally, when the huge gloomy black bear shifted from one buttock to another, I would try to use the inhaler. But it's hard to use an inhaler when you can't inhale.

Bugs Bunny

I felt like Bugs Bunny. Bugs Bunny when he's been
hit over the head by Elmer Fudd. There's a moment of
silence, where he *appears* to be completely fine. But then
hundreds of tiny cracks appear all over him, almost like
a jigsaw puzzle, and one by one the pieces fall out until
eventually there isn't enough bunny left to hold together,
and the rest falls to the ground in a cloud of dust.

I went to an acupuncturist. It turns out there isn't an
acupuncture point for feeling like Bugs Bunny.

Help

We didn't know where to turn. A friend of a friend suggested we go to see someone who was an expert in these matters.

We drove to a dark house where a German man and a German woman practised psychotherapy. Their eyebrows told me they were brother and sister.

We sat and explained the situation to the woman. Why had this happened? What did it mean?

Apparently, it meant I had not loved my baby enough and I had not bonded with him at birth. I left before my fist bonded with her face.

Godzilla

I felt like Godzilla. I felt ready to knock over buildings, kick over bridges, destroy Tokyo. I wanted to pluck helicopters out of the sky and eat them like drumsticks. I wanted to swat jets away and flick trains off bridges.

But unlike Godzilla, I'm not good at expressing anger. My anger levels range from miffed to irked. If things are really bad, I sometimes reach the cusp of rankled.

So even though I was in a towering peeve and a homicidal miff, I kept it all in. I gritted my teeth and kept smiling.

Ouch

Everything started to hurt. My limbs, my teeth, my eyes, my hair follicles. Also my stomach. The pain became so intense that I had the overwhelming compulsion to cut myself to let it out. I wanted to open my stomach and spill my guts.

I went to a homeopath. He asked me what was wrong. I said my tummy felt funny.

The homeopath asked me if I ate a lot of dairy.

And I said, no, nope, virtually no dairy because I hate milk.

No, wait, I really like cheese so yes, I eat a lot of dairy.

No, but I don't like yoghurt so on balance, probably not much dairy.

Although I do sometimes have ice cream so yes, a lot of dairy.

But I'm not mad on eggs so not really much dairy.

But I do eat a lot of butter, so yes, lots of dairy.

Then we ran out of time.

Then I lay awake all night worrying that I'd misrepresented myself on the dairy front.

That made me think: imagine if someone asked me something more profound or difficult than whether I eat a lot of dairy? How would I cope?

I still don't know the answer to the dairy question. I mean, I like squirty cream, so on balance . . .

Emergency cord

Worse than the pain in my hair follicles was the pain inside. Where was it? My brain? My heart? My soul? I didn't know where it was, just that it was unbearable.

The pain continued to get worse. If it had been in a physical part of my body, I would have gone to the doctor, I would have called an ambulance, I would have gone to A & E. But it was inside. I was an inside-out tornado. A swirling turmoil of destruction on the inside, but totally calm outside.

I stood on the Tube and stared at the emergency cord. Could I pull it for an existential crisis? I looked around at my fellow passengers and thought that wouldn't be a good idea.

I'm fine, thanks, how are you?

Inside, I was frantically pulling emergency cords, sending up flares, tapping out distress signals in Morse code, writing 'SOS' in the sand, shouting 'MAYDAY! MAYDAY!' at the top of my voice. But on the outside, I just kept smiling and smiling and smiling. And if anyone asked, I said, 'I'm fine, thanks, how are you?'

Boooooooooo!

Meanwhile, I spent some time having 'meatings' with Miranda Hart where we would eat meat and talk about how we should be talking about work. Miranda is even more lovely and charming and hilarious than you think she will be, and her dog is my soulmate.

We worked together on her series (which had the 'wit and subtlety of an aged Stilton' – Statler and Waldorf) and also on a live show. After one performance, I went backstage to say hello. The changing room at this theatre was utterly bleak. It had the lighting of an operating theatre, the curtains of a crime scene and a patterned carpet that made you question the point of life itself.

Five minutes in the company of the carpet pushed me into a bottomless pit of despair.

I said goodbye to Miranda and walked down the carpet of doom to the stage door. Maybe God (if He was still speaking to me) would give me a sign that everything would be all right. That there was hope. I opened the door and heard a thousand people's expectant intake of breath. And as I stepped out into the night, I heard the same thousand people say, 'Boooooooooo!' as they saw, not Miranda, but me.

The woodpecker

You can't get a diagnosis for autism before the age of two. I spent the next year watching The Scrap. I had now read every book on autism and scoured the internet for every piece of information I could find. I was an expert. In fact, I knew too much.

Everything he did I analysed – was that a sign he had it? Was that a sign he didn't have it? I counted down the days until I could find out.

He did that thing babies do of bending down and looking at you through his legs. And he was giggling and I was giggling but then I froze because – that's a sign. But it's also something that some babies do. It can mean everything and it can mean nothing.

Meanwhile, a friend made us a bird house in the garden. As soon as he put it up, some birds moved in. I would watch as they worked tirelessly to build a nest inside the box.

It was an unusually hot summer, so I spent a lot of time in the garden with the boys. It wasn't long before I heard tiny tweets coming from the bird box. It was a lovely sound. And the parents flew back and forth with food every few minutes. I knew how they felt; the boys ate constantly.

One day I heard a new noise from the bird box. It was a woodpecker pecking at the hole. He looked beautiful with his red crest. But he was clearly an idiot. 'Stupid bird,' I thought. 'He can't fit in the hole. And anyway, it's taken.' But he kept pecking and pecking and eventually the hole got bigger and then he got in there and he took a chick. I was devastated.

A couple of days later, I heard the pecking again. And he took another chick. And one by one, he took the chicks until there was only one chick left.

The next day, we were in the garden and I heard the pecking again. And I couldn't stand it. It was boiling hot, but I went inside the house and locked every window. I could still hear the pecking.

When I went out into the garden, the bird box was silent and the woodpecker had gone.

Scruffling

Life with The Speck felt like a tug of war. He was slipping through my fingers. He was losing words, losing interest in the world, retreating.

I was constantly trying to find the key that would unlock him.

There would be moments of connection, of joy, of progress but these would be followed by moments of despair, anxiety, retreat.

It was easier to follow him into his world, to lose yourself, to function only in ways that were meaningful to him, to exist in a bubble.

I remember someone coming to look after The Speck while I took The Scrap for his injections. She asked what The Speck liked to do. I explained that he liked banging on the radiator and scruffling plastic coat hangers through his hair. And he would only eat if you sang 'Riding Along in My Automobile' to him.

She looked at me strangely and I realised that what had become completely normal to me did not seem normal to other people.

226

Stones

The Speck had an extensive gravel collection. Whenever we went out, he would carry a bucket and spade, because you never know when a gravel-collecting opportunity might arise.

He would rush towards someone's driveway (or, one unfortunate time, someone's grave) and start digging and studying each pebble individually. He would then select only the finest stones and we would take them home in his bucket.

Every night when I undressed him, a shower of gravel would tumble to the floor. I worried that the eroding coastline of Great Britain was partly due to The Speck's ever-increasing gravel collection.

The Scrap wasn't interested in gravel. But one day, without warning, he fell in love with The Speck's spade. He gazed at it lovingly and then serenaded it with a love song (in a language spoken only by The Scrap) for about two hours.

The only time they fought was over the spade. The Speck wanted to dig with it and The Scrap wanted to sing to it.

Gravy

During this time I was asked to work with Armando Iannucci. He is a comedy hero of mine and I was staggerblasted to be asked. I worked with him on *The Thick of It*, *Veep* and *Avenue 5*.

Armando had assembled a group of uniquely brilliant writers who were a joy to work with. Once a script was written, he would ask us to come up with at least three alts (alternatives) each for various lines of dialogue. So your third suggestion might inspire someone else's third suggestion, which might inspire someone else's third suggestion – and you end up with something you would never have achieved on your own. There is something freeing about being able to suggest multiple lines. It stops you going for the 'safe' or 'obvious' line and allows you to try more unusual ideas. Armando used to explain this extremely collaborative process as 'making gravy'. You might throw in a carrot or an onion, and then when the gravy is finished, you won't be able to recognise your carrot or onion – but the gravy would not be the same without it.

On my first day on the set of *The Thick of It*, Armando decided one of the lines wasn't working and we needed something new for Peter Mannion (Roger Allam) to say when caught lying by the press. I was paralysed by fear and anxiety. And then something unexpected happened. On the brink of both passing out and having a nosebleed, I had an idea. I mumbled it – and people laughed. The other writers thought it was good. I was astonished.

'No,' said Armando. 'That's too funny.'

I looked at him, confused.

'Peter Mannion would never be able to think of an actual joke in this situation. It might be funnier if he just said as many words as possible without actually saying *anything*.'

And he was right. It was much funnier.

But the point is, I once thought of a really funny joke. About twelve years ago.

Legume

I was watching The Scrap every second of every day. But what were 'traits' and what were 'symptoms'? What was he picking up from his brother and what was coming from within? I decided he should spend more time with some (catchily named) neurotypical children so I signed him up for a Montessori nursery school.

Two days in, he came back very unhappy. He was whiny and close to tears, he didn't want to eat, he didn't want to play, even the sight of the beloved spade couldn't cheer him up. I tried everything. I wondered how I could work out what was wrong. And then I wondered if his nose had always been *that* wide. I looked up his nose. A chickpea was lodged up there.

It turned out that they had been doing some legume-based art work at nursery and he had stuck a chickpea up his nose.

I took him to the doctor, I took him to A & E, I took him to the Ear, Nose and Throat specialist. Nobody could get it out. Injuries don't get more middle-class than a legume-based art mishap at a Montessori. Yet this one was outfoxing the greatest medical minds. And the longer it went on and the longer the pointy instruments they used, the more The Scrap cried. But as he cried, hummus started coming out of his nose. It was a miracle – like water into wine. And finally, the hummus dislodged the chickpea and it was out.

The Day

It was an unusually warm day in autumn when I took
The Scrap to meet the specialist. I felt like I'd been
holding my breath for a year. Living a half-life, in
suspended animation, watching, waiting, hoping, fearing.

The Scrap and I strolled through Regent's Park. The
leaves were turning orange and red, the sun was warm,
the air was still and The Scrap was singing a happy song.
After waiting twelve months, we were almost late for the
appointment because The Scrap wanted to stop and sniff
every flower.

We entered the building and thirty minutes later we
were out.

The woodpecker had struck again.

Lemming

I wanted to cry but I couldn't. My throat hurt and my
eyes stung and my breathing came in gulps, but no
tears. Sometimes the feeling would last for days on end.
Teetering on the brink. But never falling. Like a lemming
with its foot tangled in a piece of moss.

Evil Beaver

I started to feel like I had a beaver inside me. But not
just a normal beaver. Some kind of Dark Overlord Beaver.
Gnawing at me. Slowly killing me from the inside.
Probably doing some evil poos in there too. That's the
kind of thing Dark Overlord Beavers do.

The death of the Tooth Fairy

Soon after that, The Speck lost his first tooth. That night, I crept into his bedroom holding a 50p piece. All I had to do was remove the tooth from under his pillow and replace it with the money, without waking him up. I gazed at him. He looked so beautiful and so peaceful, and there was a little smile on his lips. I leaned in. Staring at this small, grubby, slightly stinky enigma, I was overcome with such an overwhelming feeling of love, I felt like I was falling through space. I decided to give him a gentle kiss, but before I could do so, there was a noise. Plop. What was that? Did I imagine that? Plop. No, there it was again. Plop. What was making that sound? A large black spot appeared on the pillow next to The Speck. And then another, and then another. What was happening?

I looked up at the ceiling, round at the room. More and more black spots were appearing. Where were they coming from?

Oh, of course. I was having a nosebleed. As always, I was expressing my feelings through my nose.

I quickly reached under his head for his tooth and left a pint of blood on his pillow. The Speck was now lying in a bed that looked like there had been a Tooth Fairy massacre on it. I know I will inevitably scar my children for life, but this was not the way I had planned on doing it. I stood, tooth in one hand, 50p in the other, blood pouring onto my pyjamas.

I rushed out of the room. I returned with clean pyjamas and a plugged nose. *Now* all I had to do was change The

Speck's pillow case, sheet and duvet cover and wipe the blood off his cheek, without waking him up. This was a little more tricky.

I don't know if ninjas change bed linen very often – but if they do, I expect they do it very much as I did. With extreme stealth. Somehow, I managed to change all his bedding without waking him up. I am woman, hear me roar, but very quietly so as not to draw attention to myself.

I staggered back to bed and fell into a deep sleep. Only to be woken by horrified screams at dawn.

The Tooth Fairy had taken his tooth, but not left 50p. I explained as gently as I could that the Tooth Fairy almost certainly had a serious drink problem and she was probably completely wasted and had left the money in the wrong place. Look, there it is, in the bathroom, next to that suspiciously pink flannel.

Rainbows

Writing profane vitriol for a Malcolm Tucker tirade in *The Thick of It* is a good way to earn a living. At first I didn't think I would know enough swear words, but soon they were pouring out of me. It was rather unnerving.

One day, The Scrap drew a rainbow for his teacher. She was thrilled. Until she noticed some writing on the back. In that moment, I realised he had used a page from a script of mine. And as she turned the beautiful rainbow over, she was met by a barrage of profanity the like of which I don't believe she had encountered in all her years as a Montessori nursery teacher.

She looked at me, the colour draining from her face.

'Perhaps you should not stick it to the window?' I suggested.

School

By now it was time for The Speck to start school. We took
him to the local primary school. He was very excited about
this. When The Speck is excited, he lies on the floor. So
I would walk him to school and as we got to the door, he
would lie on the ground. I would then have to drag him by
his ankles across the threshold, assuring the concerned
parents that 'he's really happy' and 'he loves school'.

But The Speck didn't love school for very long. He
couldn't eat lunch there (because of the noise and the
smells), he couldn't join in PE (because of the noise
and the smells), he didn't understand what anybody
was saying and he couldn't make himself understood.
Increasingly he was excluded from activities by teachers
or other pupils. The other parents avoided us, walking
around us like we were infectious. Soon, taking him to
school felt like putting him in a cupboard. He wasn't
learning anything, he wasn't enjoying himself, he
wasn't interacting with anyone and he was becoming
increasingly anxious and withdrawn. What's more,
he was forgetting the things he did know and he was
becoming more and more distressed and unhappy. The
school made it clear they didn't want him there. His
school days lasted a matter of weeks before we decided it
couldn't go on.

Half Hulk

This made me feel angry but I was, of course, unable to express it. I remained in a permanent state of half Hulk. Desperate to rip through my shirt, burst through my shoes and hurl furniture – but stuck at perpetual uncomfy contact lens stage.

Tiny spiders

One day I was driving and (probably distracted by my inner dangling lemming) I accidentally drove onto a level crossing when my exit was blocked by a lorry. The alarm started to sound, the lights started to flash, the barriers started to come down. My car was right across the train lines. A feeling of total relief washed over me. It was the closest I'd felt to happiness for months.

But then I thought about the train driver and all the people on the train and I steered the car out of the way.

I went back to the homeopath. I told him my throat hurt.

He asked me what I was scared of.

I didn't know. Spiders?

He handed me a pill.

I looked at it and asked him if there was a tiny crushed-up spider in the pill.

He said yes.

I said I didn't think that was how life worked. You couldn't just eat things you were afraid of and stop being afraid. He disagreed.

I said you couldn't inoculate yourself against spiders by ingesting a tiny spider. He disagreed.

I asked whether, if I was scared of flying, I'd have to eat a plane? He didn't answer.

He told me to take the pill. I refused.

He told me if I wanted to get better, I would take the pill.

I did want to get better. But I didn't want to eat a tiny spider.

Glasses

I still couldn't see properly. Everything was misty. And murky. And muted. I was a smudge blundering around in a blurry world. A shadow of a ghost in a dim, dismal landscape. I went back to the opticians. They could find no reason for the blackness I saw everywhere. It was probably my age. Maybe I needed reading glasses. This plunged me further into despair. I'm old. My body's failing. I need glasses.

They told me to choose some frames from the children's section because I have an unusually small face. Fantastic. Now I'm old AND I'm a child.

'I'll just have the tortoiseshell ones,' I said, pointing.

'They're not tortoiseshell. They're covered in Gruffalos.'

The bath

We assembled a team of experts – specialist teachers, speech therapists, occupational therapists. We remortgaged our house to pay for them all. It cost a lot – not just financially but in terms of giving your house over to strangers and having no privacy.

We essentially learnt a new language – literally (Makaton) and metaphorically. We learnt how to phrase things, how to anticipate difficulty, how to negotiate, how to plan ahead, how to break things down into small steps.

We were teaching The Speck regular things such as recognising words and objects but we were also teaching him life skills.

The Speck hated baths and would scream and cry and struggle and refuse to be bathed. So we broke it down into steps. At first, we would go in the bathroom and not look at the bath or talk about the bath. We would talk about things he liked. Or sing.

Then, after a few days of this, we would go into the bathroom and maybe mention the bath in passing. We'd allude to the bath, we'd give it a significant look. After a few days of this, we would go into the bathroom and talk about the bath and maybe touch the bath. Next we would go into the bathroom and turn the tap on and then turn the tap off again. This built to filling a bath and then letting the water go, filling the bath and splashing our hands in the water, then filling the bath and The Speck standing in the water. This then led eventually to The Speck kneeling in the bath and then sitting. Finally, The Speck had an actual bath. It was a moment of triumph. But one false move and the whole process would have to start again.

Plaudits

Meanwhile, undaunted by Statler and Waldorf's relentless heckling, I decided to try a whole new medium. Theatre.

I was asked to adapt *The Snow Queen* for the stage in Southampton and Northampton. All the hamptons.

With some trepidation, I read the reviews. It was lauded as 'a confusing mess' and 'stodgy and worthy'.

However, after several weeks of searching online, I found the first good review of my career. Yes. Finally I had cracked it. 'We were able to park a five-minute walk away from the theatre and it was free to park during the evening.'

Five stars. After twenty-seven years of trying, I'd made it!

Surprises

There were plenty of other surprises too. In fact, life with non-neurotypical children (as they're catchily called) is full of surprises. Whether it's emptying out the bin so that your child can look for a piece of toenail he wants to glue back on, or getting a ceramic heart saying 'Danger! Crumbling Quarry!' for Mother's Day, or sitting out on the doorstep in the snow waiting with your son until 'the crying has gone out of my voice', or whether it's catching the boys squirting toothpaste all over the walls and then being told, 'I'm going to shave off your eyebrows so you can't be cross.'

Or whether – still on eyebrows – it's tucking a boy up in bed and being told, 'Mummy, your eyebrows are like beautiful socks.'

Or maybe it's one of them fainting (yep, passed on that excellent gene) when he hears me hoovering on Christmas Eve because he thinks it's Father Christmas's sleigh landing on the roof. Or it's comforting a child one night because he's remembered that earlier he bumped his elbow – and then comforting him again the next night because he's remembered remembering that he bumped his elbow.

Then there are surprises on a whole different level.

Chloe had been one of The Speck's teachers and had helped him learn to speak. She had then become a close family friend and now she was getting married and wanted us ALL to be there. This was a big ask and she knew it.

At first, The Speck was very anxious about the idea of going to a wedding but Chloe took photos of the venue and sent them to him. And we talked about it a lot and he approved the seating plan and I took him to choose his outfit. Even on the day, we weren't certain that he would manage it, but we drove out to the country and he was able to sit through the service. Afterwards, I assumed we'd have to leave, but The Speck was interested that lunch was happening in a tent and wanted to come and look.

We went to the tent and he is a big fan of buffets so we got some food and sat quietly at the edge, eating. Then the speeches started happening. The Speck tugged at my arm and I said, 'I know, it's noisy, we can go.' But The Speck indicated that he wanted to make a speech. I explained, no, that's for Chloe's dad and Chloe's husband and Chloe's husband's friend to do. But The Speck was insistent. He wanted a turn on the microphone. I said maybe when everyone had gone outside later, he could have a turn. He became more insistent. I said maybe we could pretend my sausage was a microphone and he could make a speech to me. He shook his head.

'What do you want to say?' I asked.

'Thank you,' he said, simply.

I tiptoed up to Chloe and explained what was happening. 'I don't think he knows what a speech is,' I said, 'and I don't think he'll be able to do it, but he wants to try.'

Chloe agreed that he should be allowed to try. So the microphone was handed to me and I explained that The Speck had something to say. The Speck made his way solemnly to the stage at the front of the marquee. He took the microphone and he stood, looking out at the hundreds of strangers watching him.

We waited.

Nothing.

'You don't have to do it,' I whispered.

The Speck didn't reply.

'You can change your mind,' I said.

The Speck didn't reply.

There was a very, very long silence.

'Are you OK?' I asked.

'I sing,' he answered quietly.

'OK. What do you want to sing?' I asked.

There was another long pause.

Then he started singing.

Come with me
And you'll be
In a world of pure imagination
Take a look and you'll see
Into your imagination

We'll begin with a spin
Travelling in the world of my creation
What we'll see will defy explanation

If you want to view paradise
Simply look around and view it

Anything you want to, do it
Wanna change the world?
There's nothing to it.

There is no life I know
To compare with pure imagination
Living there you'll be free
If you truly wish to be

We stared in astonishment. I didn't even know he knew that song. I was amazed. I was so happy and so proud. I turned to see if people were listening – and saw two hundred people sobbing. Chloe was utterly destroyed (in a good way).

I turned back, stunned, to The Speck.

'Join in!' he commanded. And then two hundred people sang it together.

Joy

Back at rehearsals with Armando for *Veep*, we were
struggling to make a particular moment work. When
Selina Meyer finally becomes president, how would Gary
(her bag man, who is utterly devoted to her) react? Would
he laugh? Would he cry? Would he scream? Would he
cheer? How would he express such extreme emotions?
It seemed obvious to me. He would have a nosebleed.
Everybody looked a little disturbed by the suggestion, but
we decided to give it a try.

As the two actors rehearsed, they made it work. It
was an incredible moment. Hilarious and tremendously
moving. The rest of us watched. People laughed, people
cried. I, of course, had a nosebleed.

Om nom nom

That winter I had to go to Scotland for the filming of another series (this one described by Statler and Waldorf as 'about as funny as inflamed piles' and 'like being smothered by cushions').

Once again, I experienced the familiar feeling of thrill and terror. As I watched the cameras rolling, the icy hand of fear crept up my backside and gripped my bowels. And I thought, 'How did this happen?'

At night, I would fall into bed, exhausted. Sleep, though one of my favourite pastimes, is hard to come by with two children.

'Wake up!' says my elder son urgently, shaking me.

Yes, my elder son, the one they said would never talk. He talks INCESSANTLY.

I sit bolt upright. 'What is it?'

'What's your favourite bird of prey?' he asks.

'I think an owl,' I say.

'OK.'

He pads back to bed.

'Mummy! Mummy!'

This time it's my younger son.

'I've made a mess on my chest!' he says.

I investigate. 'No,' I say. 'They are your nipples.'

'Nibbles?'

'Nipples.'

What seems like minutes later . . .

'Mummy, Mummy, quick! I've lost my nibbles.'

We locate his nipples and I stumble back to bed. Someone is lying in my place. It's my elder son. He carries a (filthy) Cookie Monster under his arm at all times. He asks me to explain Kim Jong-Il and Kim Jong-Un and the whole situation in North Korea, but he wants me to explain it to his Cookie Monster in the voice of Cookie Monster (so he will understand).

I hear myself say, 'Om nom nom, me have nuclear capability, nom nom,' and I think, 'How did this happen?'

I'll hold your coat

When Armando left *Veep*, the whole show was transferred to Los Angeles. A new American showrunner came on board with a room full of American writers.

I was absolutely terrified. Every single writer was a hero of mine and had written for my favourite shows, whereas I had merely smothered people with cushions. More excitingly, there were other women in the room! I cannot overstate how incredible it was to sit in a room with women writers who looked a bit like me, dressed a bit like me, had similar life experiences and attitudes and opinions – it was really, really, really, pathetically validating. It must be what it's like to be a white man all day, every day. Amazing!

Having a job that involves people bringing you food and the funniest people in the world making you laugh is just about as good as life gets. And then there was the cast. A group of outrageously talented and hilarious people.

Julia Louis-Dreyfus is something else. The greatest comic performer (in my opinion) of all time and one of the funniest and loveliest mammals I have met. A beautiful, foul-mouthed, tiny freak of a woman. It's been an inspiration to watch her make my words come alive, to watch her come up with better lines than the ones I'd thought of, and to hold her coat while she beat cancer.

Hands up

When I first had to travel to the US for *Veep*, I explained to the boys that I was going away for work. They looked confused.

'But you haven't got a job,' they said.

'I have got a job . . .' I started to explain.

'You should get a job!' they suggested, excitedly.

'No, but I've got a job . . .'

'Other people's mums have jobs!' they said.

'I do have a job,' I insisted.

They looked sceptical. I tried to explain that the thing I did on my laptop was my job.

'Solitaire?' they asked.

'The other thing I do on my laptop.'

They clearly didn't believe me.

I have always tried (and failed) to impress the boys and I suddenly saw a way that I might be able to do this.

In an act of desperation, I wrote some children's books. THIS would impress them, surely? But The Scrap did not want to read them. He said, 'I want to read a proper book by a proper writer.'

The Speck took a cursory look at them and said, 'This book is not as good as *Harry Potter*. Why can't you write a book like *Harry Potter*?'

'I don't know,' I said. 'I mean, I wanted to . . .'

'Why couldn't you write an exciting story like that?' asked The Speck.

'Well,' I stammered, 'it's difficult, I was trying to, but . . .'

'Why couldn't you write good characters like the characters in the *Harry Potter* books?' demanded The Speck.

'Well, it's not easy,' I explained. 'I was hoping that they were good but . . .'

'Hands up who thinks *Harry Potter* is a much better book than *Wilf the Mighty Worrier*?' The Speck said, appealing to the audience (The Scrap).

Both boys put their hands up.

'Hands up who thinks *Harry Potter* is exciting and *Wilf* is just silly?' shouted The Speck to the crowd (The Scrap).

Both boys put their hands up.

'Hands up who thinks J. K. Rowling is a much better writer than Mummy?' urged The Speck.

Both boys put their hands up. I also raised my hand. He made a compelling argument. I had somehow given birth to Statler and Waldorf's children.

Paaaaartay

The Speck stayed at home until he was almost eight. And
then we found a special school for him that could meet
his needs. So we moved ourselves and my parents across
London in order for him to go there.

The transformation was immediate. Being in a school
that understood him was remarkable. After one term
there, it was his birthday and he announced he would like
a birthday party. This was unexpected, to say the least. In
the past, I had tried to have birthday parties for him and
it had been a disaster – he didn't like people in the house,
he didn't like presents or new things, he didn't like cake
or singing or balloons or games. These 'parties' invariably
ended with The Speck hiding in his room and me hiding in
a cupboard trying not to cry while a group of children sat
in the kitchen wondering where the cake was.

We planned the party with military precision. Every child coming to the party had some kind of disability or special need or developmental delay. One child asked me to take photos of every room in the house and send them to her beforehand, one child asked me to take photos of all the food we would be having and send them to him beforehand, one child wanted to know the games we'd be playing, the order we'd be playing them in, the prizes and the answers to the treasure hunt, another child said he'd come but he'd just stand in the garden, and another said he'd come but he'd stay in the car outside.

The day came and the children arrived. One went and lay in our bed, fully clothed, and pulled the covers over his head, one sat by the food and ate it all, one won all the games and found all the treasure, one stood in the garden and another stayed in the car outside. At the agreed time, I brought a cake into the kitchen in total silence (The Speck had informed everyone there was to be NO SINGING), the candles were blown out and then I took the cake away again (none of them liked cake).

As the party was drawing to a close, I was heading to a cupboard to try not to cry when I heard one of the children say it had been the best party ever. Another child agreed, then another, then another. One said they were going to give it four stars on TripAdvisor.

Wearing a bloody frock

Sometimes I have to go to An Event where I am expected to wear a frock. This is a problem for me. Very few clothing lines cater for the ferret-shaped figure.

A friend of mine said that instead of buying a frock which I would only wear once, I should rent one. This seemed like a very good idea. I found a website that said 'Ten thousand dresses!' and 'A dress for everybody!' and had lots of pictures of people looking fabulous. I made an appointment, excited that I would be able to look fabulous and save money. When I arrived at the fancy Chelsea address, I discovered I had stepped into the seventh circle of hell.

The system was that I would be handed what was essentially an instrument of torture and be instructed to insert my body into a complicated tangle of scratchy, sparkly, asymmetrical torment and then emerge from the velvet cave of doom into an overly bright light where three very beautiful young women stood in judgement.

'Not quite working,' their mouths would murmur politely, while their faces shrieked, 'What the actual fuck?'

After an hour of increasingly pouffey, scalloped, strapless nonsense, they walked me to the door and said they didn't think they had anything for me.

'It should say "A dress for everybody *except* Georgia" on your website,' I suggested.

'Yes,' they replied, their eyes travelling slowly down the length of my long, long torso.

I walked away with as much dignity as an eel riding a

gerbil can muster. I felt utterly humiliated.

As I hurried away from my ordeal, I passed a shop window. There, in the window, was a frock that *wasn't* the worst thing I had ever seen. It was ridiculous, yes, uncomfortable, undoubtedly, but I could imagine enduring it for a few hours. And if I bought it right now, I would never have to think about it again. The whole humiliating nightmare would be over.

I walked into the shop. The shop assistant looked at me quizzically. She looked at everyone quizzically because she had drawn her eyebrows on too high.

I asked if I could try the dress on. She told me the changing room was busy. I said I'd wait. She sighed and handed me the dress and said I could go down to the bridal changing room.

As my trainers sank into the deep enveloping pile of the white carpet, I realised this was a very expensive shop. I made my way to the changing room, which was considerably larger than my house. I hauled the white silk curtains across and secured them with some kind of over-exuberant sash.

It was hot and airless in the bridal tomb. I started sweating as I struggled into the flouncy gibbet (which I believe is the word for those person-shaped cages they used to put people in in the Middle Ages). It was a teeny bit tight. If I could just get one size bigger I could pay and leave and this torment would be over.

The eyebrows appeared at the curtains and I asked for the next size up. She looked at me and groaned under the weight of her own disdain.

I stood in my underwear, waiting and sweating. I wanted to cry. I didn't cry, of course. Instead I had a catastrophic nosebleed. Blood gushed from my face – I looked at the white carpeted floors and the white silk curtains and the white linen chair and the white flowery wallpaper. I grabbed my T-shirt and put it to my nose to stem the flow. I sweated profusely. Liquid was leaving my body at such a rate I didn't know why I hadn't shrivelled into the human equivalent of a raisin. I really wished I would.

I prayed that the eyebrows wouldn't return. I stuffed one of my own socks up my nostril. I used my own sweat to wash my hands. I wiped my slippery body down with the curtain. I finally stemmed the flow. I heard the eyebrows approaching. The curtain parted. I leaned casually against the wall, trying to look relaxed.

'I'll take it!' I screeched in a rather high-pitched voice before she could say anything.

If her frozen face could have expressed surprise, I'm pretty sure it would have done so. She went to wrap the frock and I got dressed again, gingerly putting on my wet sock and sodden T-shirt, leaving a small bloody handprint on the wall.

It was more money than I've ever paid for anything. When the shop assistant told me the amount, my eyebrows scaled heights even hers had previously never reached. I left the shop, broke and bloodied.

Special

The conversation I had been dreading having with my son arrives. Not the one about sex. We've been over that several times and he still seems to be confused. The last time I asked him if he knew where babies came from, he said, 'A lady's front porch,' and I decided that was near enough.

This conversation starts with him saying, 'Why do I go to a special school?'

Even though I've been waiting for a question like this, I suddenly don't have a good answer. I tell him that everyone has things they're good at and things they find difficult. What does he think he's good at, or what does he find difficult? He says he's good at everything.

'Let's think about your friends,' I say. 'What are they good at, or what do they find difficult? How about Huang?'

The Speck looks thoughtful.

'He's good at being Chinese,' he observes.

'Yes he is!' I say. 'It comes naturally to him. Whereas I am *rubbish* at being Chinese. OK, how about Joseph?'

The Speck thinks again.

'He has Jewish problems,' he says.

'What are those?' I ask, slightly alarmed.

'He can't eat bacon,' says The Speck, with sympathy, because bacon is his favourite food.

'True,' I say. This conversation isn't really going to plan. 'And how about Zak?' I ask, cautiously. Zak has a condition called Proteus syndrome, which means that his face is a different shape.

The Speck thinks at length. Finally he says, 'He has a hearing aid.'

I marvel at the fact that The Speck has noticed a tiny hearing aid on what is essentially a rather unusual-looking face.

'Let's have another think about things you find difficult,' I suggest.

'This,' he says. And he gets up and leaves.

Winning

I've never thought of writing as being something I'm good at – just something that I like to do. What I am good at is standing near clever people while they do brilliant things. Specifically, Armando Iannucci (*The Thick of It* and *Veep*), Dave Mandel (*Veep*) and Jesse Armstrong (*Succession*). This has meant that I have occasionally received an 'award'. This involves getting dressed (in the bloody frock) and leaving the house, so can often feel like a punishment. However, my very limited experience of this situation has led to the following observations.

In Britain, we don't like winning. It's vulgar and embarrassing. And we don't like other people winning either. (This is why most of our sports are designed to end in a polite draw, often after five days of play.) So award shows in this country are pretty excruciating. Plus, if you are a woman you spend the evening being at best extremely uncomfortable and at worst in considerable pain due to the utterly medieval dress regulations.

In America, people love winning and people love winners. They will go on playing a sport until one team has won and the other is dead.

If you are nominated for an 'award' in America, you get driven in a fleet of limos slowly and tactlessly through the poorest areas of Los Angeles. You then pass a group of people holding homemade signs assuring you that you will burn in hell. They make a good point.

Then you arrive at the obligatory red carpet. Everyone gets funnelled into a jostling expensive walkway through a thick cloud of perfume and aftershave. And then this extraordinary thing happens. You get passed through a kind of celebrity thresher. It's amazing. I don't know how they do it and I don't know who they are. That's how good they are. But one minute, if you're me, you're walking down the red carpet jostling against Tina Fey and Amy Poehler and Amy Schumer and the next minute, you are on a smaller, dirtier, less red red carpet which has branched off from the main carpet and takes you round the back, past a few dumpsters and away from the lenses of the baying photographers. It's human winnowing.

Getting on stage is utterly terrifying. My face shakes. I didn't know that was possible. And my knees forget how to bend. And I don't know what to do with my arms. I look out, past the blur of my vibrating cheeks, at my heroes, like Tina Fey, Amy Poehler and Amy Schumer. I get kissed and congratulated by other comedy heroes, like Mel Brooks or Larry David. Everyone gets handed an unnecessarily shiny, unnecessarily pointy, unnecessarily big trophy. And then, seconds later, as I walk backstage, I pass the press area and a thousand voices shout as one, 'GET THE FUCK OUT OF THE WAY! YOU'RE RUINING THE FUCKING PHOTO!' because I have accidentally wandered too near a celebrity.

Later as I wander round, dazed and bewildered, people like Jane Fonda or Elisabeth Moss or Oprah shout, 'You go, girl!' as you pass with your pointy object.

In Britain, it is quite different. You get taken to a concrete room and shown an award. You are not allowed to touch it or take it away. Then you skulk home past the bins, in silence.

Matching

In fact, so much do Americans like winners that they have created events surrounding the event. They want to give you things for free. They have invented 'gifting suites'. There are many different levels of gifting suite. If you're rich and famous, you get given free stuff all the time. It goes without saying, I was on the bottom rung of the gifting suite. Generally speaking, I am too English and too mortified to be given free things. But one year my Canadian friend Anna announced she was coming with me and that her mum wanted free stuff.

It was an excruciating experience.

It took place in a Beverly Hills Hotel. Clearly, their system was to write to everyone who had been nominated for any of the awards and then hope that famous people would turn up. When I showed up with my unfamous face, the disappointment was palpable.

First everyone is given a 'hostess' (mortifying) and the hostess is given a bag to put all your free things into. Then you are taken round a large room full of displays where very attractive young women recite a spiel for their product with an enthusiasm that no homemade room scent (or whatever it is) could actually deserve. I felt so agonised that I just made the situation much worse than it needed to be for everyone involved.

Anna, on a mission, accepted everything. Except, because we weren't famous, the attractive young women didn't really want to give us the homemade room scent. So a polite tug of war – much like you see at a six-year-old's birthday party – would ensue. Once you have been given a gift, you have to have your photo taken. I imagine many, many photos have been deleted which showed an attractive young woman smiling resentfully while I stood next to her, looking like some kind of tortured hostage.

Towards the end of the ordeal, we approached a display of homemade lotions. An attractive young woman launched dutifully into her spiel.

'We have some anti-ageing cream . . .'

'Oh good!' I said, feeling the morning's events had aged me considerably.

'For your vagina . . .' she continued.

I pondered on this for a moment. As far as worrying about things is concerned, I thought I had everything covered. But a whole new avenue of anxiety had just opened up before me.

'Do you have anti-ageing cream for the face?' I asked.

'No,' she answered.

'Because I feel like they need to match. I can't have a tired old face and a youthful vagina. If anything, I'd rather it was the other way round. In a typical week, more people see my face than my vagina.'

I didn't take the cream. Too English. Too embarrassed. And I just didn't want that photo out there, in the world.

And that, dear reader, is why I have a wizened old vagina. In case you were wondering.

Lump

The boys were defying the odds, defying the experts, defying the woodpecker. The Scrap was thriving at mainstream school, The Speck was achieving things we'd never thought possible. I was being given shiny pointy things and offered anti-ageing cream for my vagina – the zenith. And yet, while everything life-wise and work-wise couldn't have been better, I was feeling worse and worse.

I felt like I was being slowly digested by a giant black snake. I was just a me-shaped lump in the snake. My voice seemed small and muffled. There was no escape. I'd been swallowed whole. I just had to wait for the digestive juices to do their work.

My dreams got worse. In every respect. I dreamed that I was alone, drowning in a sea on the moon. I would try to pull myself out, but my hands would just grasp clumps of nothing and I would slide back into the blackness.

Shatter

My head was full of thousands of confused moths flapping and thrashing around and bumping against my skull.

The Witch has a unique way of dealing with moths. She sprays hairspray at them. They turn shiny and stiff, they stop flapping and they glide gracefully to the ground, where they shatter.

I don't advocate cruelty to moths, but I longed for these turbulent moths in my brain to glide and shatter and leave me in peace.

Body snatcher

I felt like an imposter. Like I had pulled on some ill-fitting skin and was doing a really bad impression of myself. Most worrying of all, people were falling for it.

I went to a healer. I couldn't think what else to do. I'm not sure why it is supposed to be healing to sit in a room while someone makes (bad) guesses about your life.

She got my name wrong.

She said I had a cat (I'm allergic).

She said there was a Maggie in my life (nope).

She said I had a close relationship with someone called Charlie (also no).

I stumbled out, feeling queasy with self-loathing.

As I went home, I felt like I was picking my way through the debris of my life, while disintegrating with every step. Buckling under the weight of regret, remorse and disgust.

Being an alien

Sometimes life takes you somewhere truly unexpected. Out of the blue, I was asked to go to the White House to write something for Julia Louis-Dreyfus (the fictional Veep) to film with Joe Biden (then the actual Veep). This was filmed secretly to surprise President Obama and involved Michelle Obama and Nancy Pelosi.

Joe Biden had just come back from Ukraine. I asked his chief of staff how Ukraine was. She said, 'Far! And it was a long day, and then at the end of the day we had to say, "No, you can't have our guns!" Awkward!'

This final word also involved jazz hands.

Biden then proceeded to tell me some secret information about sanctions until his chief of staff suggested meaningfully that he change the subject (while whispering to me, 'Please don't tweet that!').
He did change the subject. Noticing I was English, he changed the subject to how much his mother hated the English. His parents were Irish and she had written several poems about her hatred of the English. He went off to find them and returned with hundreds of poems describing how God must smite the English and rain blood on our heads. He also told me that when his mother visited the UK she had stayed in a hotel where the Queen had once stayed. She was so appalled that she slept on the floor all night, rather than risk sleeping on a bed that the Queen had slept on. I admire anyone whose principles come between them and a comfy bed.

Later, Biden gave us a tour of the Vice President's

Residence. It is astonishing. I went to the bathroom and there were lots of plastic cups and napkins saying 'The Vice President's Residence'. I stuffed as many as I could into my bag and went back to join the others.

'You need to go to the bathroom,' I whispered urgently to Julia. 'I've just been there, now *you* need to go.'

'OK,' said Julia, rolling up her sleeves, 'what did you do?'

It's touching that the greatest living comedy performer of our times was totally prepared to go and wipe up my shit, and also touching that once I'd explained, she was all in for pinching cups and napkins.

We spent three days walking the corridors of the White House. They could have done with a lick of paint. We went into the Oval Office, which was glorious. We went down to the kitchen, where we filmed with Michelle Obama. Michelle Obama's 'people' had vetoed a lot of the lines we'd written. But Michelle herself was up for anything. She was funny, charming, wise and had perfect comic timing. She kept encouraging me to write more lines. I would write something in biro on a scrap of paper and say, 'Will you say that?' and she'd say, 'Sure!' and then deliver it perfectly.

The concept of the short film was that Biden and Julia would have a sort of *Ferris Bueller's Day Off* experience while everyone else in Washington was at the Correspondents' Dinner. We had them finding the key to the White House under a flower pot and letting themselves in. We also had them raiding the White House kitchens and eating junk food and going to get matching tattoos.

When we were filming in the downtown tattoo parlour, I was standing with Joe Biden, Julia and Nancy Pelosi. A Secret Service agent opened the door, looked at me and said, 'Secret Service?' and then nodded and left again. I have never been so thrilled in my whole life. She thought a small, puny, tired-looking woman was Secret Service!

Julia said, 'Oh, we're all dead then,' but I didn't care, I felt invincible! I felt like Wonder Woman. I spent the rest of the day whispering things into my sleeve until Julia finally whispered into my sleeve, 'Shut the fuck up.'

Hanging out with the First Lady of America and the First Lady of Comedy was not something I ever thought an anxious girl from Elephant and Castle would do. What's more, in order to be allowed to work there, I'd had to get a visa. What was printed on the visa was probably the nicest thing anyone has ever said about me: 'Alien with extraordinary ability'. If you'd told me that's what I'd grow up to be when I was eleven, I'd have taken that.

Being an alien

Meanwhile, I felt like an alien in other ways. Or more specifically like John Hurt in the film *Alien* when something is about to burst out of his chest. I could feel the thing pounding inside me, trying to get out. I could feel it pushing against my ribs. I could feel that any second now, it was going to erupt out of me, splattering entrails and gizzards all over the soft furnishings. But it didn't come. It was stuck. It pounded and it hammered and it paced and it flailed but it couldn't escape. It was trapped. An alien stillbirth.

I found myself longing to look down and see the drooling, jagged-toothed monster explode out of me and go skittering across the floor. Maybe then I would feel better.

Marbles

I felt worse. Like a ghost, I drifted around. Absent from the world but too present. Unable to leave, unable to stay.

I was desperate for sleep. I longed for oblivion. I would stare at the stars. At the blackness. At infinity. I felt as if I was being sucked into a black hole.

The light I could see from the stars had been travelling for hundreds of years. The stars might even be dead now. I felt as if I was dead, but still somehow transmitting some long-out-of-date light into the world. And nobody had realised I was gone.

I could almost hear the plink, plink as, one by one, each of my marbles rolled slowly away. I was down to single figures. What's more, I'd lost the ability to wrangle my own marbles. What was I going to do?

The last resort

Killing yourself is an intrinsically dramatic act. It's
tricky if you are not a dramatic person. What is the
most discreet and inconspicuous way of ending your
life? Without upsetting anyone or drawing attention to
yourself? This was a conundrum I could not solve. I didn't
want to make a fuss.

As a very last resort, before I chose how to make my
exit from the world, I decided to see a doctor.

'My mess is a bit of a life right now,' I mumbled. 'I mean,
not that . . .'

She indicated that I should elaborate. But I couldn't.

I couldn't speak. The words wouldn't come. They were
there but they were out of my reach. She referred me to a
therapist.

The not talking cure

I went and I said nothing. I didn't know what to say, I didn't want to say anything and even if I did want to say something, the alien and the moths and Godzilla and the Dark Overlord Beaver made it impossible.

An idea

After weeks of silence, I was losing hope.

Her: How are you?
Me:

I tried to speak, but the moths were flapping furiously in my brain, the alien was pounding on my chest, Godzilla was stomping all over my inner Tokyo and the Dark Overlord Beaver was tucking into my intestines.

Her: Can you tell me what's going on?
Me:

The moths began bombarding and ricocheting inside my skull, the alien had acquired some kind of enormous mallet, Godzilla was roaring and obliterating my inner Tokyo and the Dark Overlord Beaver was now gorging on my innards.

Her: Can you tell me how you're feeling?
Me:

I summoned all my strength to reply and took a deep breath in. The moths suddenly stopped flapping; the alien stopped mid-pound; Godzilla stood, helicopter drumstick in hand and foot hovering over a building; the Dark Overlord Beaver put down my lower intestine. They all cocked their heads and listened to what I was going to say next.

I swallowed. I breathed. I swallowed and breathed. Triggering a coughing fit. Godzilla rolled his eyes. The Dark Overlord Beaver and the alien exchanged a weary look. A moth tutted. And they all resumed what they were doing.

Her: Are you anxious about anything?

I nodded.

Her: Can you tell me some of the things that worry you?

I shook my head.

Her: Maybe you could write them down . . . ?

And so I did (see page 1).
And it helped. Thank you.

Thank you for listening. It turns out that sometimes it's easier to tell things to strangers.

It means that I've been able to release Godzilla and the Dark Overlord Beaver and the alien and the moths into their natural habitat. They didn't want to be imprisoned in a puny human. And it's better for me that way. They still bother me sometimes. But other times, we just hang out.

Acknowledgements

Thank you to my agent Jo Unwin who suggested I write this and who I told, in no uncertain terms, that I would absolutely not be doing so.

Thank you to Louisa Joyner, Libby Marshall, Kate Ward and everyone at Faber – without you this book would be mainly about hamsters. It remains to be seen whether that is a good thing or a bad thing.

Thank you to Holly Ovenden who draws how I wish I could draw, and who somehow knew what a Dark Overlord Beaver looks like.

Thank you to Julia Louis Dreyfus, Jen Crittenden and Gabrielle Allan Greenberg for being brilliant, hilarious and inspiring friends.

Thank you to the Material Girls for thirty years of laughter and for being wonderful women before it was trendy to be a woman.

Thank you to Francesca Gardiner, Adam Countee, Anna Beben, Simon Braine and Milly Reilly – for being early adopters of what I consider 'writing' and what I consider 'a book'.

Thank you to Lily Williams for finding some pieces of writer lying around, sewing them together and bringing them to life, thereby creating the monster that I am today.

Thank you to Frank Rich for friendship, food and adventures.

Thank you to my Beloved Potatoes.

Thank you to all the funny, brilliant, talented writers I've sat with in various small windowless rooms. You have taught me everything I know. Thank you for making me laugh till biscuit crumbs flew out of my nose. And thank you for understanding I have to have lunch by 11 a.m.

Thank you to Armando Iannucci for life changing gravy.

Thank you to Marilyn Imrie – I miss you.

Thank you to Phil Whelans for being one of the funniest and best humans.

Thank you to Matt for continuing to charge me very reasonable prices for my Christmas stocking.

Thank you to Catherine Bailey – you know and understand me even better than my Amazon algorithms.

And finally thank you to Mum and Dad for being my favourite double act and my best audience.

And thank you to my boys, for everything.